LEON BATTISTA ALBERTI

Books in the RENAISSANCE LIVES series explore and illustrate the life histories and achievements of significant artists, rulers, intellectuals and scientists in the early modern world. They delve into literature, philosophy, the history of art, science and natural history and cover narratives of exploration, statecraft and technology.

Series Editor: François Quiviger

Already published

LEON BATTISTA ALBERTI

The Chameleon's Eye

CASPAR PEARSON

REAKTION BOOKS

For Maria

Published by Reaktion Books Ltd
Unit 32, Waterside
44–48 Wharf Road
London N1 7UX, UK
www.reaktionbooks.co.uk

First published 2022

Copyright © Caspar Pearson 2022

Printed and bound in India by Replika Press Pvt. Ltd

A catalogue record for this book is available from the British Library

ISBN 978 1 78914 521 2

COVER: Matteo de' Pasti, medal with winged eye (reverse), *c.* 1446–50, bronze. National Gallery of Art, Washington, DC (Samuel H. Kress Collection, 1957.14.648.b).

CONTENTS

Introduction

eon Battista Alberti is a central figure in the history of the Italian Renaissance but one who is difficult to know. A writer and intellectual, he was unusual in combining his literary activities with a strong interest in the visual arts, authoring treatises on painting, sculpture and architecture and even, in later life, turning to architectural practice himself. From the outset, this has led to a certain hesitancy regarding who Alberti really was and how he should be assessed. Famously, he came to prominence in modern times when he was lauded by Jacob Burckhardt, in his *The Civilization of the Renaissance in Italy* of 1860, as the 'universal man': a heroic, many-sided figure whose faith in reason and his own talents made him the consummate Renaissance individual. On the other hand, the art historian Julius von Schlosser, writing in the 1920s, considered Alberti to be all sides and no centre: a non-artist and a fraud who excelled at nothing in particular.[1] Notwithstanding these polarized opinions, which embody an ambivalence going all the way back to Giorgio Vasari's sixteenth-century biography, it was mostly Burckhardt's view that would hold sway for a hundred years. Only in the 1960s, when the Italian scholar Eugenio Garin discovered some previously unknown writings, did a major

---

1 Unknown artist, *Leon Battista Alberti*, 15th century, pen and ink on paper.

reassessment take place. As a result of this, Alberti emerged as a much stranger and more unknowable figure than had previously been supposed: a dazzlingly original writer deeply engaged with moral and existential questions who produced works full of irony, dissimulation and wild, bizarre fantasy. It is this Alberti who in recent decades has been the object of a huge proliferation of specialist studies that, alongside new critical editions and translations, have made his works more available and more deeply analysed than ever before.

The general shape of Alberti's life has been well established ever since Girolamo Mancini published the first edition of his monumental biography in 1882. Italian scholars have continued to lead the field but there are some excellent accounts of Alberti's life in English. Joan Kelly-Gadol's important book of 1969, *Leon Battista Alberti: Universal Man of the Early Renaissance*, contributed much to the understanding of Alberti's technical undertakings and to the contextualization of his activities within the broader epistemological concerns of the Renaissance. Mark Jarzombek's highly original *On Leon Baptista Alberti: His Literary and Aesthetic Theories* provides a fertile reading of Alberti that remains indispensable today. Meanwhile, Anthony Grafton's major biography, *Leon Battista Alberti: Master Builder of the Italian Renaissance*, employs its unmatched erudition brilliantly to illuminate the world of Renaissance humanism as well as many aspects of Alberti's thinking.

In this biography, I have sought to create a short introduction to Alberti that takes account of some of the key ideas advanced in recent publications. For the sake of accessibility and concision, I have cited modern English translations of Alberti's works whenever they were available, and have not included original language quotations. Constraints of space have led me to focus closely upon Alberti himself, with only limited exploration of historical context. Moreover, I have had to be selective. Some of Alberti's works are not considered, and some are treated only briefly and very partially. Certain aspects of his life, such as his career at the papal curia, do not receive sustained attention. While it does move broadly chronologically, the book is ordered thematically. In this way, I hope to give an overview of some of Alberti's main concerns and to provide a starting point from which those who are minded to do so can explore further. With Alberti, there is always another summit just over the horizon.

ONE

Exile and Return

In the hot summer of July 1436, after sixteen years of construction, the dome of Florence cathedral reached completion (illus. 2). The cupola crowned a building that the Florentines had always intended should outshine every other cathedral in Tuscany. They had begun their project at the end of the thirteenth century, and over the next hundred years had continued to work out and refine the design. As the fourteenth century progressed, the Florentines began to envisage a cathedral with a magnificent dome resting on an octagonal base with an internal diameter of more than 44 metres (144 ft) at its broadest point, raised over the crossing (the part of a church where the nave and transept meet). In its size and height, the cupola would surpass ancient precedents at Hagia Sophia in Constantinople and at the Pantheon in Rome. Projecting a dramatic profile, reminiscent of the domes of Persian and Timurid architecture, it would stand tall upon a high drum, and on the exterior its curvature would take the form of an acute fifth, a type of pointed arch often used in gothic building. As the fourteenth century gave way to the fifteenth, much about the cupola's appearance had thus already been decided, but its construction was another matter. So high was the dome, and so great was its span, that it was

2 Cathedral of Santa Maria del Fiore, Florence.

impossible to rely on the traditional method of building using 'centring' (a kind of wooden supporting scaffolding that holds the masonry in place and stops it from falling in before the structure has been completed). Surmounting this problem required a vast collective effort, but there can be no doubt that its resolution depended especially on one person. Filippo Brunelleschi, a goldsmith by training who worked as a sculptor, architect and engineer, invented a method of building that required no support of any kind whatsoever. On this basis, the Florentines embarked on construction in 1420, and to those who saw the building go up, its steady rise must have seemed something close to a miracle.

One such observer was Leon Battista Alberti, a 32-year-old scholar, expert Latinist and papal bureaucrat. Alberti had been in Florence since 1434, the year that an uprising prompted Pope Eugene IV to flee from Rome. Disguised as a Dominican friar, Eugene was forced to cower ignominiously in the bottom of a boat as he sheltered from the hail of stones hurled by an angry mob. Having escaped, he sought refuge in the Tuscan city, and gradually his entire court – the papal curia – relocated there with him. For Alberti, it was something of a homecoming. His family hailed from Florence, though for many years they had been excluded from the city, for reasons that we will see below. He had been there before, at least by 1430, in order to take possession of a benefice granted to him by his papal employers at San Martino a Gangalandi. Consisting of a church and some adjoining lands, from which Alberti could draw an income, it was located high in the hills outside the city. From there he would have had an excellent view of Florence and of the dome that was becoming, each day, an ever-more dominant feature of its skyline. In his regular travels around the city, meanwhile, he would have seen the cupola close up, taking in not only the structure itself, but the enormous works surrounding it: the teeming building site, the heavy lifting machines and the huge supplies of stone, brick, wood and iron that flowed in and contributed to its making.

It is small wonder that all of this had a strong effect on Alberti, for he was deeply preoccupied with the visual arts. In fact, not long after his arrival in Florence, he wrote a short treatise, *On Painting*, or *De pictura*, which he solemnly recorded having completed at a quarter to nine on the evening of 26 August 1435. Over the following year he continued to revise this text, in which he sought to provide a sound theoretical basis for the making of pictorial art, and on 17 July 1436 he sent a copy to Brunelleschi, attaching a brief introductory letter. Perhaps he was caught up in the excitement of the moment, with the cupola just weeks away from completion. In any case, the letter brims with enthusiasm, lavishing praise upon Brunelleschi, whom he addresses familiarly as Pippo (short for Filippo), and lauding his achievement as a feat of great historical import:

> What man, however, hard of heart or jealous, would not praise Pippo the architect when he sees here such an enormous construction towering above the skies, vast enough to cover the entire Tuscan population with its shadow, and done without the aid of beams or elaborate wooden supports? Surely a feat of engineering, if I am not mistaken, that people did not believe

possible these days and was probably equally unknown and unimaginable among the ancients.[1]

Yet for Alberti, the significance of the cupola was not only technical and world-historical but personal, as he makes clear in the first part of the letter:

> I used both to marvel and to regret that so many excellent and divine arts and sciences, which we know from their works and from historical accounts were possessed in great abundance by the talented men of antiquity, have now disappeared and are almost entirely lost. Painters, sculptors, architects, musicians, geometers, rhetoricians, augurs and suchlike distinguished and remarkable intellects, are very rarely to be found these days, and are of little merit. Consequently, I believed what I heard many say that Nature, mistress of all things, had grown old and weary, and was no longer producing intellects any more than giants on a vast and wonderful scale such as she did in what one might call her youthful and more glorious days. But after I came back here to this most beautiful of cities from the long exile in which we Alberti have grown old, I recognised in many, but above all in you, Filippo, and in our great friend the sculptor Donatello and in the others, Nencio [Lorenzo Ghiberti], Luca [della Robbia] and Masaccio, a genius for every laudable enterprise in no way inferior to any of the ancients who gained fame in these arts. I then realised that the ability to achieve the highest distinction in any meritorious

activity lies in our own industry and diligence no less than in the favours of Nature and the times.[2]

Florentine art and architecture, Alberti suggests, had converted him from a fundamentally pessimistic outlook, in which history appeared as decline, to a fundamentally optimistic one in which it appeared as progress.[3] Moreover, this broader historical view seems to have been inextricably bound up, in his mind, with his own personal and familial history, with the readmission to Florence of the Alberti family after the 'long exile' in which he says they had 'grown old'. Perhaps, as he gazed up at the cathedral on a warm July evening, with swallows darting through the sky and the distinctive tones of the Tuscan dialect filling his ears, the cupola appeared to him as a symbol of his restoration to the city to which he belonged; the healing of a dreadful wound that for decades had troubled not only him but every one of his relatives. It was an injury from which he had suffered throughout his entire life, one that was inflicted long before his birth and that had only started to heal eight years earlier, in 1428. On 29 and 30 October that year the governing councils of the Florentine Republic had issued a set of provisions annulling all ordinances hitherto published against the Alberti, finally ending the family's exile and paving the way for their return to their ancestral home.[4] To understand just what this meant, we will have to look back to the events of the thirteenth century and consider the rise, fall and rehabilitation of the Alberti clan.

EXILE

The first exclusions of male members of the Alberti family occurred in the 1380s, with the expulsion from Florence of Leon Battista's grandfather Benedetto di Nerozzo Alberti and Benedetto's cousin Cipriano di Duccio. Both were leading figures on the political stage. Florence was governed as a republic, according to a constitution instituted in the late thirteenth century that allowed for the distribution and frequent rotation of offices among the city's guildsmen. In this system, power was concentrated especially in the hands of a group drawn from the members of the seven major guilds: the judges and notaries, the merchants of cloth, wool, silk and of fur and skins, the bankers and money-changers, and the physicians and pharmacists, with varying degrees of participation granted to lesser guilds at different moments in history. Under this arrangement, the elite, a sort of pseudo-nobility of 'great' families referred to as the *grandi*, was forced to share power with the *popolo* (people), a distinctly urban class of merchants and lawyers. It was a markedly inclusive form of government for its time, although it only included those belonging to the restricted group of males over the age of thirty who were deemed eligible for public office.[5] It was also competitive and, despite the outlawing of political parties, it was characterized by intense alliances, enduring enmities and factional struggles.

Under this regime, the Alberti had prospered. The first of their clan to establish himself in the city was one Rustico, who settled in Florence towards the start of the thirteenth century.[6] His family were lords in the area of Catenaia – wild, mountainous lands lying to the north of Arezzo, in a region

3 Alberti coat of arms in the Oratorio di Santa Caterina delle Ruote, Ponte a Ema.

known as the Valdarno Casentino. Rustico's predominantly city-dwelling descendants in the succeeding centuries would proudly bear the family's coat of arms, displaying four taut chains (*catene* in Italian) meeting in a central ring, referring to the clan's aristocratic origins in these Catenese territories (illus. 3). In Florence, Rustico prospered as a jurist, a path followed by at least a further two generations of the family. Indeed, for most of the thirteenth century members of the clan were referred to in Florence as 'del Giudice' (literally 'of the Judge'), a name that gave way, at the start of the fourteenth century, to 'Alberti del Giudice' after a prominent member of the family called Alberto, and was later shortened simply to 'Alberti'.[7] To have a surname at all was a mark of distinction, helping to indicate that the Alberti were prominent members of the elite.

Then, as now, there were riches to be had from the law. But also then as now, banking offered even greater rewards, and it was from this profession that the Alberti would ultimately acquire their enormous wealth. They had managed to escape censure when, in 1293, a regime dominated by the *popolo* branded many *grandi* 'magnates' and excluded them from public office. Shortly afterwards they began to build their business. The first of the Alberti companies was founded in 1302. Specializing initially in the importing and refinishing of cloth, and subsequently in the local manufacture of woollen cloth, they gradually came to oversee a web of international commercial interests in which finance played an ever-increasing role. Prudent management steered the Alberti through some choppy waters: above all, the financial crash of the 1340s, which was partly occasioned by the default of the English king Edward III on vast loans from Florentine financiers.[8] The drastically over-extended banks of the Bardi and Peruzzi families, with which the Alberti business was closely intertwined, found themselves horribly exposed and collapsed.[9] However, the Alberti survived the fallout and continued to build an international network of banking houses, dividing, in 1346, into two companies, and then, in the subsequent generation, into multiple companies, but keeping ownership of all their businesses within the bounds of the extended family.[10] Papal finance, which was by its nature international and which required complex financial instruments in order to conceal the practice of usury, was particularly lucrative, and the Alberti won a considerable share in it. Such was their success that when Messer Niccolaio di Jacopo Alberti died on 7 August 1377, the chronicler Guido Monaldi remarked that there had been no wealthier man in Florence for the last two hundred years. Describing Messer Niccolaio's lavish funeral, which was held the following day in the Franciscan basilica of Santa Croce, Monaldi reckoned that it cost around 3,000 florins.[11] He might have been exaggerating (one could buy a decent house for 150 florins), but his point is clear.

ALBERTI ASCENDENCY

Such wealth brought the family to prominence both at home and abroad. Indeed, well into the fifteenth century, following their period of exile, and when the family business was already on the wane, an English Act of Parliament imposing a special tax on foreign bankers in London could refer to

'Albertyns' along with Venetians, Catalans, Prussians and others, as though the Alberti constituted a nation in and of themselves.[12] In Florence the family became ever more visible in public life. The ruling body of the government, the Signoria, was constituted of eight priors, who held office for a period of two months, led by a ninth who held the position of Gonfaloniere di Giustizia (who acted almost as the head of the republican state). In all, Alberti men served as priors 48 times and as Gonfaloniere nine times: a clear indication of their intensive participation in political affairs and of their highly elevated social status.[13]

In the factional world of medieval Tuscany, taking sides was inevitable. The lords of the mountain strongholds in the Catenaia, from whom the Alberti were descended, had originally been supporters of the Holy Roman Emperor (and would soon come to be known as Ghibellines). However, even before they entered Florence, Rustico's branch had become upholders of the rival authority of the papacy (and were later to be termed Guelphs), and had changed the colour of their coat of arms from red to blue to signify their new allegiance. In the thirteenth century, as Guelphs and Ghibellines struggled violently for supremacy, the Alberti participated in the conflict and were forced, in 1260, to flee from Florence for a period of six years, during which time their Ghibelline enemies destroyed their palaces.[14] By the mid-fourteenth century, with the Guelphs having long triumphed, the Alberti allied themselves with the Ricci family, whose faction leant towards the *popolo*, meaning in practice that they favoured somewhat wider participation in the government and defended the traditional role of the guilds in the constitution.[15] Ranged against them was the conservative faction of the Albizzi, which sought to concentrate power in the hands of a smaller group of elite families who were closely allied to the Guelphs, and to diminish the power of the guilds.

The political ascendency of the Alberti arrived in the 1370s and was occasioned by an extraordinary event: the revolution of the Ciompi (wool workers) in 1378. Although short-lived, the Ciompi revolution paved the way for a popular regime that opened the government to the participation of many minor artisans and labourers: the so-called *popolo minuto* who had previously been assiduously excluded by both the *popolo* and the *grandi*.[16] Benedetto di Nerozzo and Cipriano di Duccio Alberti were early supporters of the new order. They prospered under it and ascended to high office. Indeed, Benedetto was knighted in 1378.[17] However, when the Ciompi fell and the Albizzi faction resumed its dominance in 1382, both men became vulnerable. Not that they were defeated immediately; their downfall was, to paraphrase Ernest Hemingway, gradual, then sudden. Their unsurpassed wealth and influence ensured that they could continue as major political players for some years to come, but in 1387 they miscalculated. That year, Benedetto's son-in-law, Filippo Magalotti, was appointed Gonfaloniere di Giustizia, to the general horror of the Alberti's enemies. When it transpired that Filippo was underage and thus not eligible for office, Benedetto tried to strong-arm the appointment through.[18] These tactics backfired spectacularly, with the result that not only was Filippo denied office, but Bardo Mancini, a loyal partisan of the Albizzi and implacable enemy of the Alberti, was appointed in his place. Bardo succeeded in immediately summoning a *balìa* (a temporary,

extraordinary committee with wide-ranging executive powers), which he asserted was needed to bring the republic back
to order.[19] This left the Alberti dangerously exposed.

THE ALBERTI EXILE

From that point matters progressed quickly. Understanding
that he had been outmanoeuvred, Benedetto sought to limit
the damage. Writing to the *balìa*, he signalled the end of his
political ambitions by petitioning to be excused from public
office. Citing age and infirmity, Benedetto asked that he
might be left to attend to his personal affairs and his spiritual
wellbeing. The petition was granted immediately and a number of further provisions were added. Not only Benedetto but
his kinsman Cipriano would be excluded from office. Further-
more, both were banned, on pain of a 1,000 florin fine, from
entering the buildings housing all of the main organs of government (the palaces of the Signoria, Podestà, Captain of the
People and Executors of the Ordinances of Justice). The following day, 6 May, every Alberti male, with the exception of
the sons of Messer Niccolò Alberti, was excluded from office
for a period of five years. Moreover, Benedetto and Cipriano,
who had requested permission to leave the city to attend to
their businesses, were now ordered to remove themselves
from Florence within eight days. Before eighteen days had
passed they were required to be no less than 160 kilometres
(100 mi.) away and they were to remain at this distance for
two years.[20]

  These were the first in a series of exclusions and other
moves against the Alberti that took place over the next

quarter of a century. In 1393 five Alberti were expelled from
the city and others were excluded from office. In 1400 three
Alberti sons-in-law were executed and six Alberti men were
sentenced to death in absentia for conspiring against the
republic. In 1401 all of the male members of the family over
the age of sixteen were banished, after a further conspiracy
was uncovered. One of them, Antonio, was subjected to an
enormous fine of 3,000 florins. All were given punishments
requiring that they absent themselves from the city at certain
distances and for fixed periods of time: some at 160 kilometres
for ten years, others at 300 kilometres (180 mi.) for twenty
years, and others still at 500 kilometres (300 mi.) for thirty
years. Further conspiracies of 1411 and 1412 led to still more
drastic penalties, including one execution and the placing of
a bounty on the heads of several Alberti men, who could now
be killed for reward within a 320-kilometre (200 mi.) radius
of the city. Meanwhile, any Florentine citizen transacting
business with an Alberti company was subjected to special
taxes and other burdensome restrictions.[21]

Importantly, these exclusions did not signal an end to
relations between the Alberti and the Florentine republic.
On the contrary, those who were exiled from the territories
of the state remained firmly within the grasp of its administra-
tion. From the outset, Benedetto and Cipriano were required
to produce and dispatch to Florence fortnightly notarized
reports attesting to their whereabouts. When the general exile
of 1401 fell upon the Alberti males, their Florentine properties were sequestered and the revenues were used by the state
to pay an allowance to both the exile himself and any wife or
children remaining in the city. Over the following decades,

exiled Alberti corresponded with the Signoria over a number
of matters, asserting their rights to undergo taxation (an
important recognition of their continuing citizenship), nego-
tiating over the fate of their Florentine properties and
requesting changes and exemptions to the conditions of their
bans. Alberti women remaining in the city played a particularly important role, ensuring the family's continued presence
and sometimes going to court to defend their interests.[22]

In some ways, the Alberti were well-positioned for exile.
They controlled a vast, international web of financial interests
and their banks had branches in many parts of Italy and Europe.
Their businesses survived their exclusion from Florence and
continued to prosper.[23] Throughout their banishment, mem-
bers of the family fell back upon this commercial network,
often taking up residence at its major and minor nodes. Thus,
during their exile, Alberti men are recorded as having died in
Vignone (Piedmont), Genoa, Brescia, Mantua, Padua, Venice,
Modena, Bologna and its surroundings, Forlì, Rimini, Iesi,
Antona (near Carrara), Sutri (Lazio), and other locations in
Friuli and the Marche, as well as in London, Bruges, Paris,
Montpellier, Rhodes, probably Cyprus and at sea while trav-
elling to Flanders.[24] Nonetheless, however extended the space
through which the family moved, it was one that was centred
on, and largely structured around, the city of Florence. It was
from Florence that the bureaucracy that ordered their lives
emanated, to Florence that they dreamed and schemed to
return, and around Florence that they orbited at fixed
distances.

In the years 1403–4, towards the beginning of the Alberti's
general exile, Leonardo Bruni, who would soon become the

Chancellor of Florence, composed a panegyric to the city in which he described the hierarchical organization of its territories as a series of concentric circles:

> Just as on a round buckler, where one ring is laid around the other, the innermost ring loses itself in the central knob that is the middle of the entire buckler, so here we see the regions lying like rings surrounding and enclosing one another. Within them Florence is first, similar to the central knob, the centre of the whole orbit. The city itself is ringed by walls and suburbs. Around the suburbs, in turn, lies a ring of country houses, and around them the circle of towns. The whole outermost region is enclosed in a still larger orbit and circle.[25]

In somewhat similar fashion, one might imagine a different set of concentric circles: those described by what Randolph Starn has termed the 'contrary commonwealth' of exiles, orbiting at their given distances around the central buckler of Florence.[26] Dispersed and displaced, the exiles nonetheless continued to inhabit a space that was hierarchically organized from the centre, their lives caught in a strange game of push and pull with a city that simultaneously kept them at a distance and held them close.

BATTISTA ALBERTI

It was into this complex situation that Battista Alberti was born. A recently discovered horoscope, one of several written out in Alberti's own hand, has allowed scholars to date the event precisely: he was born at around 3 a.m. in Genoa, on Monday, 18 February 1404. His father, Lorenzo, the son of Benedetto di Nerozzo, had been exiled in the general ban that fell upon the Alberti males at the turn of the century. Forced to stay at a distance of at least 300 kilometres (180 mi.) from Florence for a period of twenty years, he later became subject to the harsher penalties of 1412. While in Genoa Lorenzo fathered both Battista and his brother Carlo (long considered to be the older brother but now believed to be younger) with a woman whose identity has not been securely established. A document that names her as Bianchina di Carlo Fieschi, a noble widow who died of plague in 1406, is probably a modern forgery.[27] Whoever Alberti's mother was, Lorenzo did not marry her, and nor did he take any measures to legitimize his two sons.[28] Instead, in a manner typical of others who were banished, he waited until he could marry a Florentine woman of good family, something that he achieved in 1408 with his wedding to Margherita Benini, the sister of another exile.[29] No doubt Lorenzo hoped that Margherita would provide him with legitimate Florentine heirs; the marriage was childless, however. Battista was thus born in Genoa into the condition of exile, the illegitimate son of a (presumably) Genoese woman. Nonetheless, he was named Battista after Florence's patron saint, John the Baptist, and he grew up, in Genoa, Venice, Padua and Bologna, within a distinctly Florentine, and indeed Albertian, milieu.

With all of this in mind, one can well imagine that in the summer of 1436, after two years of residence in Florence, in the midst of a moment of artistic flourishing, and in possession of a benefice that ensured his financial independence, Battista Alberti must have felt a great sense of achievement. His grandfather Benedetto had died far from home on the island of Rhodes, and his father, Lorenzo, had breathed his last in Padua fifteen years before. He, however, had returned to the ancestral city, winding his way from the periphery back to the centre. Once there, he encountered the immense structure of the cupola, which perhaps presented itself to him as the very innermost circle of the spatial order in which the Alberti moved; a place of wonder that stood as an apt image of the kind of 'making whole' and triumphing over adversity that he had always sought.

Perhaps. And yet, while the letter to Brunelleschi undoubtedly speaks to the joy of his acquaintance with Florence, there is much that it does not tell us. It is, after all, a highly rhetorical construction, written in a laudatory tradition and following laudatory conventions. Like many of Alberti's writings, it appears increasingly subtle and multi-layered the more one considers it. His comparison of geniuses with giants, for example, is ambivalent to say the least, since the latter were strongly associated, in both ancient myth and biblical scripture, with the worst kinds of hubris and moral turpitude. The letter was far from Alberti's last word on Florence. He was already sharply critical of many aspects of its culture and society, and he would wrestle for his entire life with feelings of alienation and estrangement regarding his *patria*. In that sense, he remained always an exile. In part it was a condition that could not be overcome, and in part it was one that he held dear. Undoubtedly he was aware that a long Tuscan tradition connected exile with the making of literary meaning. The most prominent exponents of this practice were Dante and Petrarch, writers who not only mined exile for its poetic potential but associated it strongly with the very condition of authorship, finding in banishment – both real and imagined – the kind of distancing upon which an authorial identity could be fashioned.[30] Like them, Alberti would hold fast to the notion of his exile, visiting and revisiting it throughout his works, ever performing the delicate balance of positioning himself at both the dead centre and the far periphery of the world in which he lived.

It should also be acknowledged that we know nothing at all of Alberti's real relationship with the artists that he mentions in the letter, and there is not much profit in speculating about them. Considering the great time that has elapsed, the many documents likely to have been lost, the verbal exchanges never captured and the infinite complexity of human interactions – such that our understandings of relationships even between people we know well are often partial and misguided – there is simply not enough evidence to judge. Whether one relies upon the letter itself or imputes significance to the lack of any surviving written response to it, the argument cannot be decisive. Brunelleschi might have received it warmly or regarded it with cold contempt. Perhaps he embraced Alberti, and the two of them drank long into the night as they discussed their shared intellectual interests. Perhaps he walked right past Alberti without any idea of who he was, barely thinking of him from one moment to the next. We simply cannot know. What can be said is that Alberti was, from an early stage, engaged with architecture, that he imputed enormous significance to it and that he was inclined from the start to link it with moral and historical issues of enormous import. Whatever the true state of his relations with the artists he mentions, the letter undoubtedly demonstrates his desire to connect with people who operated in a very different field from his own and who possessed a set of skills and knowledge that were in many ways foreign to his usual practices. For even if he was an intimate of the visual artists, Alberti was not one of them. Rather, he was a writer. Indeed, he was one of the most extraordinary and original writers of the entire Italian Renaissance.

TWO

Blossoms and Scorpions

t the start of the 1440s Alberti composed a dialogue in which the speakers consider how best to avoid the anxieties and doubts that constantly assail the human mind. The *Profugiorum ab erumna libri III*, which might loosely be translated as 'On Avoiding Mental Anguish', records a fictional conversation between three characters based on real people. The main speaker is Agnolo Pandolfini, a member of one of Florence's most prestigious families. Agnolo was an elder statesman of the Republic, but he had by this time withdrawn from political life, spending many of his days at an extensive country property located just a stone's throw from Alberti's benefice at San Martino a Gangalandi. His interlocutor in the dialogue is Niccola di Vieri de' Medici, a scion of Florence's dominant family, though not belonging to its governing branch. The third character is Battista – Alberti himself. He remains mostly silent throughout the dialogue of which he is in fact the author.

This group of friends partakes in a three-day discussion that ranges across three books. The first is set within the cathedral of Santa Maria del Fiore, beneath the recently completed dome. In the second the characters stroll through the streets of Florence. In the third they return to the cathedral

and stand outside of it. As they traverse this grand theatre
of human activity, Agnolo and Niccola ruminate upon some
central questions in moral philosophy, drawing, in the process,
on a wide range of ancient literary sources. Agnolo's discourse
is shaped by the ideas of Roman moral thinkers such as Cicero
and Seneca, as well as poets like Ovid and comic playwrights
such as Terence. It is redolent throughout of the Stoic tradition of Roman philosophy, although it is not written in Latin
but in the Tuscan (Italian) dialect. It also encompasses some
major works of Greek literature, returning time and again to
themes from the poetry of Homer. Brought together in this
way, these citations form a complex whole; an erudite assem-
blage that is governed by a layered and constantly varying
process of allusion and evocation.

To a receptive reader, it is a gripping display, and the characters themselves are no less enthralled. When, in the third
book, Agnolo laments that his speech is disorderly, Niccola
denies that it is anything of the sort. On the contrary, he
finds Agnolo's discourse to be as finely wrought as one could
wish. To demonstrate how, he embarks upon an extended
simile that is both architectural and pictorial in nature, liken-
ing the composition of a speech or a piece of writing to the
creation of a mosaic floor. Speculating on the origins of such
mosaics, Niccola suggests that they might derive from the
Temple of Artemis at Ephesus, a building that was traditionally numbered among the Seven Wonders of the Ancient
World. Constructed by the entire population of Asia, over
a period of no less than six hundred years, the temple was,
Niccola says, extraordinary to behold. Its walls were built from
'huge pieces of marble hewn from mountains', its columns

were immensely tall, its roof was made from gilded bronze, and it was decorated, inside and out, with great slabs of porphyry and jasper. When the building was completed, every part of it shone forth wondrously – all except for the floor, which remained 'naked and neglected'. Therefore,

> in order to adorn the floor and to make it stand out from the other surfaces in the temple, they took the little left-over pieces of the marble, porphyry, and jasper that had been used throughout the structure, and, fitting them together according to their colours and shapes, they composed various pictures, thus covering and dignifying the entire floor. In this way, they created a work that was no less pleasing and well received than the great ornaments adorning the other parts of the building.[1]

Something of the same kind, Niccola argues, occurs in the composition of speeches and writing. All of the arts and disciplines, he says, were invented over many years by the greatest minds of Asia, and Greece above all. In so doing, those ancient sages

> constructed, in their writings, a sort of temple and home for Pallas Athena [the goddess of wisdom] and for Athena Pronaia, the goddess of the Stoic philosophers. They built the walls from the investigation of truth and falsehood, and made the columns from the observation and understanding of natural forces and effects. Above this, to defend the whole work from

adverse weather, they placed the roof: a roof made from
the skill required to flee the bad and to seek and desire
the good, to hate vice, and to want and love virtue.

This metaphorical temple was also a generator of mosaics.
Indeed, Niccola says, 'when I want to ornament some small
thing that I have made for my own private enjoyment, I take
from that noble, public building whatever I consider suited to
my designs, and, dividing it into little pieces, I distribute it as
I see fit.' From this practice, he asserts, there arises a saying,
which he quotes in Latin: *Nihil dictum quin prius dictum* (nothing
is said that has not been said before). 'One sees many people
use these literary motifs,' Niccola observes, 'incorporating them
into and scattering them throughout their many writings.
Consequently, all that is left to writers these days is to collect
and sort these elements, and then put them together in a way
that differs from what others have done and that suits their
own purpose. And in so doing, they behave almost as though
they were imitating the maker of that first mosaic.'[2]

    This provides a powerful image of literary composition as
a fundamentally intertextual process in which fragments of
ancient texts are continually put to new uses. It may sound
rather negative – a disavowal of even the possibility of orig-
inality – but it is not as simple as that. When such a literary
mosaic is well made, Niccola says, when 'I see the parts joined
together so that they all conform, in their colours, to a certain
prescribed and delineated shape and picture, and when I see
that there are no spaces between the parts, no unsightly gaps,
it delights me and I think that one could not wish for anything
more.' Agnolo, he continues, has brought together what was

previously dispersed, and has made of it a new and coherently structured whole: something that he judges to be not only 'rare and marvellous' but 'almost divine'.

Of course, this praise is ultimately self-reflexive. The words that are spoken by Agnolo and Niccola in the dialogue are in reality those of Alberti himself, the author whose wordless avatar stands listening respectfully to his two older companions. Indeed, just prior to this passage, Alberti introduces the third book of the *Profugiorum* in his own voice, making an apology for the disorderly nature of his text before returning to the dialogue itself. His apology is almost immediately mirrored by Agnolo's, and the attentive reader is aware that in addressing the latter, Niccola also addresses the former. In other words, Alberti here reveals something of his method and draws our attention to the sheer complexity of his literary feat.

Roberto Cardini has suggested, in an influential analysis, that we find here the key to understanding Alberti as a writer.[3] Those of his contemporaries with sufficient education to see it would have been aware that a complex game of allusion and citation was at play within his works. They would have recognized it because they commanded a commensurate level of erudition and because they too were writers, engaged in a similar process. This restricted public was made up of scholars of a very specific type. Like Alberti, they belonged to an elite, avant-garde intellectual movement, although one that was not formally constituted or named at the time of its existence. Today it is known as humanism.

HUMANISM

The nature of humanism continues to be the subject of much debate, but some of its broad characteristics may be outlined here.[4] At the root of all humanist practices lay a deep fascination with Greek and Roman antiquity. Humanists were captivated by the sense that antiquity was both close at hand and profoundly distant. The collapse and disappearance of ancient societies, whose ruins were conspicuous across much of Italy, posed complex questions about history and the workings of time. Antiquity could seem both startlingly familiar and exotically foreign. On some occasions, ancient writers described a relatable daily life and discussed ethical questions with which a fifteenth-century reader could easily identify. On others, they spoke of pagan rituals and vast imperial building projects that were barely imaginable. Antiquity was by turns both intangible and graspable; it was lost and yet it might be recovered. And the humanists believed that the means for that recovery lay within their chief preoccupation: language.

At the heart of humanist practices was the recuperation of Latin eloquence. Already in the fourteenth century, a number of scholars had become increasingly conscious that the Latin of their own age – the Latin of churchmen, notaries and academics – was not the same Latin used by the ancient authors they admired. The language of orators such as Cicero, playwrights such as Terence and poets such as Virgil was altogether richer and more versatile. Examples could be found in surviving ancient texts but even those texts allowed for only a fragmentary understanding. To recover the Latin of ancient Rome would require remaking it piece by piece through the efforts of many scholars working across generations. It is this task that the humanists took on. It might seem to us a dry undertaking, technical in nature and narrow in scope. Yet it was motivated by strong passions. To achieve a high level of Latinity was to communicate directly with the deceased writers of a far-distant era; to come as close as one could to assimilating that long-vanished world. It was to open up whole realms of philosophy, poetry and history. It provided the key to a dazzling intellectual universe.

The humanists' project was to enter that universe. In many ways, it was a project of desire; one that was born, like all desire, from the distance between the desiring subject and the object to which its attentions are directed. In common with many other attempts at linguistic recovery, it was also, and more urgently, a powerful instrument for the shaping of the present. The humanist preoccupation with eloquence led to an intense focus on rhetoric, the ancient art of speaking well. While medieval scholastic philosophy depended upon logic, the humanists were interested above all in verbal persuasion. From the start, their new form of eloquence was embraced by the rulers of Italian city-states, who quickly recognized its potential to support authority, legitimize regimes and undermine enemies. As Coluccio Salutati, a pioneering humanist who was also a politician and diplomat, and who served as the Chancellor of the Florentine government between 1375 and 1406, put it: 'It is certainly a great thing to embellish one's writings with words and ideas, but the greatest accomplishment, and indeed the most difficult, is to bend the souls of one's listeners as one wishes by means of a polished and weighty oration.'[5]

Salutati wrote this passage in praise of Petrarch, who had been his friend and mentor. Petrarch was a key figure in establishing a humanistic culture in Italy.[6] He had spent many years in Padua, where he helped to foster a humanist tradition that still remained vital when the exiled Florentine merchant Lorenzo Alberti moved his family there in the early fifteenth century. In fact, Padua was one of the foremost centres for humanist education in Italy. It was home to a school run by Gasparino Barzizza, who also lectured in rhetoric at the city's *studium* (or university). Barzizza was a modest and genial man as well as a formidable scholar with a particular interest in Cicero. His house was a hub for the exchange and copying of manuscripts, and he kept an extensive Latin library. For forty gold ducats a year, pupils could attend the boarding school that he ran from his home, where they would acquire competence in Latin and enter into the complexities of grammar and rhetoric, as well as some aspects of philosophy.[7] Fees of this kind were loose change to a man like Lorenzo, and he sent both of his sons to study with Barzizza, perhaps as early as 1414. There, they were immersed in a highly sophisticated intellectual milieu. University students seeking further instruction mingled with the younger pupils, and Barzizza's many scholarly acquaintances often passed through. This connectedness kept the school at the cutting edge. The early fifteenth century was an age of literary discovery in which intrepid book hunters unearthed a wealth of ancient manuscripts that had languished for centuries in monastic libraries. Often, when these long-lost tomes emerged into the light of day, Barzizza was able to gain rapid access to them and incorporate them into his teaching.

It was a highly stimulating environment for an academically gifted pupil like Alberti. His subsequent move to the University of Bologna was less successful. Bologna was widely considered to be the foremost university in Europe for legal studies, and was the destination of choice for many of Barzizza's students, who subsequently entered legal careers. In Alberti's case, such a path would have continued a family tradition that extended all the way back to his first Florentine ancestor, Rustico. However, Bologna's large faculty must have seemed quite alien after the intimacy of Barzizza's house. The curriculum was punishing, demanding that students mastered both canon and civil law and requiring the rapid assimilation and memorization of a large corpus of legal texts.[8] Alberti struggled fully to embrace his legal studies.[9] After leaving Bologna, he did not become a lawyer. Instead, he worked at the papal court in Rome, where he put his Latin to good use drafting documents such as bulls and briefs. This position afforded him a stable income that allowed him to pursue a career as a writer. It was a path on which he had already set out when, as a twenty-year-old student in Bologna, he took some time out from the laborious task of memorizing legal codes to author his first literary work: a play titled *Philodoxeos fabula* (The Tale of Philodoxus).

PHILODOXEOS THE PLAY

Philodoxeos is written in Latin, in imitation of the comedies of Roman playwrights such as Plautus and Terence. A clunky moral allegory with a laboured plot – in Anthony Grafton's words, 'a creaky clockwork device designed to produce the right moral at the right time' – it tells the story of Philodoxus (lover of glory), who seeks to wed Doxia (glory) while fending off his rival Fortunius (fortunate), the son of Tychia (fortune).[10] Other characters, who assist on one side or the other, are similarly titled so as to spell out their roles as personifications. Significantly, their names (at least in the final iteration of the text) are almost all Greek, something that points to a further aspect of the burgeoning scholarly culture in which Alberti participated. The study of Greek was a growing field of interest among the humanists. In 1397 the Byzantine scholar Manuel Chrysoloras had come to Florence from Constantinople at the invitation of Coluccio Salutati and had taught Greek there for five years. Some of his pupils went on to become humanist educators in their own right and disseminated Greek studies across the Italian peninsula and beyond. Barzizza does not seem to have had Greek works in his library, and there is no evidence that he possessed an advanced knowledge of the language. Other members of his circle, however, did. For example, one of Chrysoloras's students, Guarino da Verona, who would go on to teach Greek at his own school in Ferrara, was a close friend of Barzizza and a frequent visitor to Padua during the period in which Alberti was there. Another humanist competent in the language, Francesco Filelfo, who was also a Barzizza alumnus, was in Bologna while Alberti was resident in the city. Later, Alberti's friend Lapo da Castiglionchio the Younger would write that he took up the study of Greek in Bologna on Alberti's suggestion, perhaps indicating that he was also a student of the language at that time.[11] However he did it, Alberti seems to have acquired some reading knowledge of

Greek, and certainly his works contain frequent allusions to Greek sources.[12]

In several respects, then, *Philodoxeos* is an exemplary humanist work. Its language is Latin, and it also demonstrates some knowledge of Greek. It is set in Rome, but some of its characters, including Philodoxus himself, are Athenians. It thus encompasses the two major poles around which the humanists had structured their antique imaginary. Replete with jokes about classical philosophy and rhetoric (schoolboy humour for Barzizza-trained schoolboys), it seems designed to appeal to scholars who had been drilled through the humanist curriculum. However, the play did not announce itself as such. *Philodoxeos* was deliberately a fake. Alberti did not initially acknowledge it as his own, but instead passed it off as an ancient comedy by a playwright called Lepidus (meaning 'witty'). The play did the rounds as such for over a decade, until Alberti prefaced it with a new commentary and claimed it back, adding more Greek content and making the tone more sober and serious.

What was his motivation? Perhaps he wanted to submit himself to the ultimate blind peer-review, testing his ability to 'pass' among the razor-sharp, hyper-Latinate, antiquity-revering humanists. If the recuperation of ancient Latin was those scholars' primary goal, what could be better than to produce something that even they could not distinguish from a Roman original? Yet alongside the desire to show that he could cut it, there is perhaps also a more polemical intent. *Philodoxeos* demonstrates mastery of the Latin language and one of its genres, but it also destabilizes the authority of antiquity. When he revealed that what had been admired as an ancient work was in fact modern, Alberti raised questions about cultural values – questions that he was quick to high-light when, in his later commentary, he wrote contemptuously of those who retracted their praise of the work once they realized that he was the true author. Alberti's sleight of hand was in fact both a thoroughly humanist display and a means of wrongfooting pretentious readers; simultaneously an homage to ancient literature and a reproach to those who automatically considered antiquity to be superior to moder-nity. From the very beginning, therefore, Alberti's writings hinted at an incipient critique of humanism; a critique that would be given clearer voice in his next substantial piece of prose writing: *De commodis litterarum atque incommodis* (On the Advantages and Disadvantages of Letters).

THE TROUBLE WITH SCHOLARSHIP

The *De commodis* is a short treatise that examines the joys and sorrows of scholarship. Its date cannot be determined with certainty, but it may have been finished as early as 1428, towards the end of Alberti's studies in Bologna. Affecting a tone of studied weariness and cynicism, the treatise constitutes a sustained polemic regarding the hardships of the scholarly life. Learning is characterized as a tyrannically demanding activity that allows its victims neither respite nor pleasure. Travel, festivity, relaxation and hobbies of any kind are barred to the scholar, who must remain chained to his books like a prisoner to a rock. To achieve erudition, Alberti observes, takes a lifetime, and the odds of making a success of it are minuscule. Nor are any rewards forthcoming, unless one is prepared to sell out entirely. Only corrupt lawyers and political lackeys will profit from their learning. If honest scholars hope for wealth or civic honours, then they are horribly deluded. This litany of suffering and humiliation occupies almost the entire treatise, and only at the very end does Alberti change direction. In the final paragraphs, he assures the reader of his own devotion to letters and speaks of the sacrifices that he has made in order to pursue them. It is not his intention to dissuade people from their studies, he says, but rather to urge them on. They must, however, proceed on the understanding that they cannot expect any transitory rewards and should think only of virtue.

The treatise thus appeals to the idea of a pure form of intellectual activity that is carried out for its own sake and without any instrumental goals, other than perhaps the general one of helping all of humanity by producing knowledge. Using the rhetorical device of prosopopoeia, in which the speaker gives voice to another person or object, Alberti has the scholar's books themselves deliver a long speech about the excellence of learning. In the end, then, scholarship achieves its victory. But the victory is far from emphatic. Readers depart with Alberti's laments ringing in their ears, and the final paragraphs are not sufficient to drown them out. We hear his formal conclusions and we might accept that they are indeed his views, and yet we cannot free ourselves from the crushing weight of his foregoing pessimism. Our confusion is further heightened by what seems to be an unrelenting irony that pervades the entire treatise. Alberti's denunciations are often hyperbolic, sometimes comically so, and readers cannot escape the sense that they are at one and the same time meant, and not fully meant – or rather, not meant consistently for everyone, everywhere, always. We leave, then, not with the sense that matters have been resolved, but rather with the sense of a puzzle whose solution continues to evade us.

SCHOLARS IN THE WORLD

Anybody who works in academia will easily recognize many of Alberti's complaints. His characterization of scholarship as incompatible with money-making, his sense that it is under constant attack from instrumentalizing forces that seek to undermine it and his conviction that its rewards are incommensurate with the effort, that it does not receive the esteem it deserves, that it impedes the forming of personal relationships and that it is tyrannically all-consuming are all still standard fare in discussions among university faculty. Appeals to a higher ideal of scholarship and the conviction that one is surrounded by charlatans and sell-outs – be they managerialist deans or egotistical showboats – remain common. At the same time, the diligent young students that Alberti describes would be entirely at home in a 1980s John Hughes high-school movie, in which they would all be played by the young Anthony Michael Hall. Caricaturing them as a bloodless breed of library-dwelling nerds, Alberti suggests that their lack of practical aptitude is matched only by their social ineptitude:

To take just a few examples, who does not see at weddings, concerts, singing groups, or young people's games how scholars are looked on with scorn and even hatred? Everybody thinks it becoming in a young man to play the lyre, to dance, and generally to practice the pleasing arts, and people consider these appropriate activities for the young. Those who are even moderately skilled in such arts are generally welcomed and are popular. If they are credited with some such ability, they are invited and asked to join in. But not the young scholars, *they* are pushed away and excluded. If they show their wan faces at such occasions, people consider them either ridiculous or burdensome, and if they try to participate, how they are laughed at and what disparaging remarks they get to hear! Who doesn't look down on a singing or dancing scholar?[13]

These scholars have the feel of stock characters, and yet the reader cannot but wonder whether they articulate some trace of personal experience. Lapo da Castiglionchio the Younger, who had known Alberti since their days together at Barzizza's school, later recalled that his friend had had no time for childish fun even when he was a youngster.[14] In *De commodis*, certainly, the scholar's existence is a lonely one in which social encounters often end in humiliation. This is particularly true where romance is concerned, to the extent that Alberti advises that marriage will not be possible:

Do not invite comparison of a poor fellow with a wealthy one, nor of your pale and gloomy countenance with that of other young men. Do not expect your authority to matter to a girl more than good looks. Go away, flee, hide yourself in a library. An athletic, handsome, attractive, and charming young man will make sure with all his skill and ingenuity that you do not take away his beloved. You'll be laughed at, graceless and poorly clad scholar, if you compete in matrimonial matters with a nicely groomed and polished lover. And if you show up pomaded and painted, you will lose all the authority and dignity of a man of learning.[15]

Perhaps these are the laments of a young man who has learned the hard way that, in courtship, his clever lines about Cicero's use of the superlative are no match for an adept dancer with cool hosiery and a brand-new lute. More broadly, however, the passage points to one of Alberti's chief preoccupations in these years: love.[16]

LOVE

It seems that from the very outset, love appeared to Alberti as a fierce and intractable problem; one that was (perhaps counterintuitively) closely bound up with the question of scholarship and writing. His first work, *Philodoxeos*, narrates the love of Philodoxus for Doxia, and while the latter is something of a cipher, with a small speaking part that consists mostly of virtuous platitudes, the former is full of passion; passion that makes him so loquacious that his ally Phroneus (meaning 'wise') keeps having to tell him to shut up.[17] Indeed, Philodoxus is so deranged with love, and so overwhelmed with anxiety, that he seems unable to make rational decisions or manage his own affairs. Without Phroneus to help, one feels that he would quickly meet with disaster. Of course, Philodoxus is no ordinary lover. He is the lover of glory

(Doxia) and as such may be identified with the humanist scholar. In that sense, his all-consuming passion reflects on the desire that dwelt at the heart of the humanist enterprise – and it does not necessarily reflect well. Philodoxus, we might conjecture, is right to love glory, but he perhaps loves in the wrong way, or loves too much, and is unable to see matters clearly.

The devoted intellectual described by Alberti in the *De commodis* finds himself in a similar position. 'I won't remind you', says Alberti (as he does just that), 'how great is the anxiety experienced by those who long for praise, who want to surpass all rivals or at least to be surpassed by none.'[18] And here we discover the real reason why the man of letters cannot sustain a love affair: like the lover of a woman, he is subject to a form of totalizing *philía* (love), and the one *philía* is necessarily exclusive of the other. That is to say that each one – the love of a woman and the love of letters – is a form of monomania that possesses its subject completely and allows no room for anything else.

This idea about love is explored at greater length in another early work, entitled *Deiphira*. Probably penned around the same time as *De commodis*, it is the first love dialogue of the entire Renaissance.[19] The speakers are Filarco, whose name suggests love of power, and Pallimacro, whose name means pale and emaciated. The two of them discuss the latter's love for a woman, Deifira, whose name denotes a warlike nature.[20] Both participants agree that the situation is a complete catastrophe. Pallimacro is consumed by love to the point where his life has been derailed. Deifira at first encouraged him but now treats him with disdain; nonetheless he is constrained by a power outside of himself to remain devoted to her. He is fully aware that this 'troppo amare' (excessive loving) constitutes a form of servitude that will ultimately wreck all of his hopes and ambitions. Yet he cannot free himself from it. Filarco, saddened to see his friend reduced to such dire straits, points out his madness, enumerates all of the errors that lovers make and suggests a number of possible remedies. But to no avail. Finally, the pair agree that the only solution is for Pallimacro to flee. Distraught, the lover takes his leave, saying, 'Farewell, my homeland, farewell my friends. Pallimacro, too faithful and too devoted a lover, shall flee to unknown lands to live there, weeping, in exile . . . Farewell, my Deifira. I am going into exile and I don't know if I will ever return.'[21]

Pallimacro thus appears rather like the writer who, according to a poetic tradition discussed in the previous chapter, must ultimately embrace exile in order to stay true to his all-consuming passion (in Pallimacro's case a woman, in the case of the writer his vocation and his thirst for glory). And just as this passion is, for the lover, a terrible burden from which the rational part of his soul yearns to be free, so the scholar is also caught in a dizzying cycle of desire and fear that can bring him only sorrow. As Alberti says in *De commodis*, 'no ecstatic pleasure and light-hearted soaring can seize you if you partly desire the huge burden of study and partly are afraid to put it down.'[22] Indeed, Alberti repeatedly describes the scholar, in his treatise, as pale and unhealthy ('pallimacro' in the truest sense) and notes that he is 'as much confined as if serving a life sentence'.

Not that love must always fail. In the months that followed the *Deiphira*, Alberti returned to the theme in a short work

entitled *Ecatonfilea* (The One Hundred Loves), in which an older
woman of experience delivers a soliloquy advising younger
women about their romantic lives. They must, she says, love
wisely and faithfully, fully but not excessively, and always
avoid falling into suspicion – the very thing that had wrecked
Pallimacro's happiness. Again, we might detect a correlation
with scholarship; something that, as we see in *De commodis*, can
go awry in an almost infinite number of ways, but that can also,
if approached with pure good faith and guided by wisdom
(just as Phroneus guided Philodoxus), confer the highest of
rewards.

ALBERTI'S HUMANISM

Love and letters, then, are at the forefront of Alberti's early
work, where they seem to be tied inextricably together. Sometimes we find Alberti ruminating upon the first while fully
immersed in the complexities of the second. Thus his short
work *Amator* (The Lover), of around 1432, is built upon a complex web of citations that demonstrates a complete command
of the entire available corpus of Latin elegiac poetry.[23] Ancient
Roman elegy was a form of verse characterized by first-person
narration and often focusing on the sufferings, and sometimes
the pleasures, of love. Among its chief practitioners were
Tibullus, Catullus, Propertius and Ovid. Alberti was familiar
with all of them and deployed them with aplomb throughout
his text. *Amator* is an early example of an Albertian textual
mosaic – one in which the literary complexity seems somehow to reflect the charged nature of the amatorial subject-
matter. However, Alberti did not simply use this material to

inform his prose writing. He also composed elegies himself.[24] His poem *Mirzia* is a long lament addressed by a man to a disdainful and ungrateful lover, while in his *Agilitta* a female character rebukes herself for falling prey to suspicion and behaving cruelly towards the man she loves. In addition to these, Alberti tried his hand at other ancient poetic modes, including eclogues – love laments with a pastoral or bucolic context. In his *Corimbus*, the title character wanders, lovesick, through the woods, while in *Tirsi*, two young shepherds, Tirsis and Florio, tell of their sorrow at being spurned by their beloveds.

In these early years, then, Alberti was a writer of both poetry and prose. He also made use of two languages: Latin and the vernacular Tuscan (commonly referred to as the *volgare*, or 'vulgar tongue'). Of the works mentioned thus far, the play *Philodoxeos*, the treatise *De commodis* and *Amator* are all in Latin. However, the love dialogue *Deiphira*, the *Ecatonfilea*, the elegies, eclogues and other rhymes that Alberti produced in this period, and the *Profugiorum* are in Tuscan (although characteristically he gives them titles derived from Latin and Greek). This dual-language approach to writing was by no means unprecedented. What *was* unusual was Alberti's habit of using the vernacular for genres that hitherto had been almost exclusively Latin. There are previous examples of vernacular eclogues but they are rare. Alberti's Tuscan elegies are perhaps the first of their kind. The point may seem trivial, of significance only to a few specialist philologists, but it is important. Alberti would champion the *volgare* throughout his life; something that, as we will see, would set him at odds with the dominant humanist culture in Florence and beyond. He seems to have intuited from an early age that a new form of vernacular literature – philosophical in character, grounded in social realities, and often taking the dialogue form – might find a non-scholarly and less Latinate readership among the merchants and civic functionaries of the Italian city-states.[25] Whether such readers really existed in significant numbers is a matter of debate. Nonetheless, from the first years of the 1430s until the end of his career, Alberti produced a series of works that appear to be aimed at them. These texts render philosophical speculation more accessible to a general reader by situating it within the world of lived experience. Simultaneously, they perform a dizzyingly complex game of citation that would have appealed (and indeed been visible) only to the most erudite scholars.

If this attitude regarding the vernacular was unconventional, it should be acknowledged that Alberti was also highly original in his use of Latin. Intertextual methods were common to all the humanists, who maintained a constant dialogue with their ancient forebears as well as with each other. However, Alberti engaged throughout his career with an unusually wide range of sources, including not only high literature but technical writings. This affected the content of his works by broadening the range of citations and introducing unexpected material.[26] It also affected his style. When writing in Latin, Alberti did not set out primarily to imitate the language of Cicero, the ancient orator and statesman who was widely considered by the humanists to represent the gold standard for Latin eloquence. Rather, despite his intense admiration for Cicero, Alberti aimed to produce an altogether more eclectic and original form of prose.[27] On the one hand, this

betrays some ambivalence about imitation as an end in itself.
He had, after all, already shown that he could mimic a Roman
comedy when he was just twenty years old. On the other hand,
he seems to have been sceptical of both the feasibility and the
value of attempts to recover ancient Latin eloquence, observing in the preface to *De commodis* that 'We cannot hope, by great
application to study, to attain the glory of ancient eloquence
and elegance; even if we tried for a long time with all our
powers, we could attain only mediocre success.'[28] That statement is ostensibly a rather conventional expression of humility
before the achievements of the ancients. Read another way,
however, it constitutes a summary dismissal of one of the central planks of the entire humanist project, and this points to
another fundamental aspect of Alberti as a writer: he was both
a humanist and a vigorous critic of humanism.

Throughout his career, Alberti subjected many aspects of
scholarly practice to unsparing interrogation, and he used his
literary skills in order to do so. This has led some modern
scholars to argue that Alberti was in reality a kind of anti-
humanist. Timothy Kircher, for one, sees Alberti as determined
to disrupt the notion that eloquence could be equated with
the moral good, a position that is implicit in much humanist
writing. To this end, he argues, Alberti frequently deployed
a fierce irony; one that exceeded, in its depth and complexity,
anything that might be found in the works of his contemporaries.[29] Its purpose was to unsettle the reader's relationship
to the text, rendering passive reception impossible and forcing
an acknowledgement of moral freedom.

Certainly, a thoroughgoing irony is visible in Alberti's
writings from the outset. When, for instance, he remarks, in

De commodis, that 'hunchbacks, people with running sores, twisted dwarfs, dolts, stutterers, men without spirit, and all the generally incompetent and non-competitive are deemed to be scholars', his hyperbole comes as a jolt and alerts us to his ironic intent, opening up a distance between the text and the reader.[30] Alongside this irony, Alberti often deals in ambiguity, simulation, dissimulation and ambivalence. Many of his writings are marked by a complex authorial self-reflexivity. His fashioning of a character based upon himself in the *Profugiorum ab erumna* and his invention of the ancient comic writer Lepidus as the author of *Philodoxeos* are just two examples.

Beyond this, however, Alberti can frequently be found questioning the very nature and worth of writing and scholarship. The anxiety that motivates such manoeuvres is already at work in all of the early texts discussed in this chapter, including those that purport to be only about love. When towards the end of the 1430s Alberti wrote his autobiography (anonymously and in the third person), he confessed that 'letters sometimes delighted him so much that they seemed like flowering blossoms from which hunger or weariness could hardly distract him; yet at other times they would seem to be piling up under his eyes, looking like scorpions, so that the last thing he could do would be to continue looking at books.'[31] This conflicted attitude found expression not only within his literary works but in the whole of his practice as an intellectual. Unusually for a humanist, Alberti sometimes sought meaning outside of scholarship as well as within it, examining practical and technical matters that were well beyond the purview of most scholars. Occasionally he appears to want to escape from language altogether, even as he is entirely immersed within it. In these instances, he says, he would occupy himself with other things, including art. Having considered his formation as a writer, we might now do likewise and turn to a work that is in many ways exemplary of his intellectual peregrinations: the treatise *On Painting*.

THREE

Painting

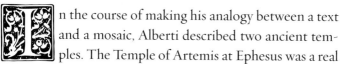n the course of making his analogy between a text and a mosaic, Alberti described two ancient temples. The Temple of Artemis at Ephesus was a real building, one of the Seven Wonders of the Ancient World. The second temple was purely metaphorical – a philosophical edifice with walls made from logic, columns wrought from natural philosophy, and a roof fashioned from ethics. Wisdom and Stoicism were enshrined within. Imaginary temples also appear in some of Alberti's other works, including the short dialogues, allegories and moral tales that he composed as entertainments to be read between courses at dinner, known as the *Intercenales*. In one of these, entitled *Paintings*, he describes a magnificent temple in the land of the gymnosophists (Hindu ascetics known from ancient literature). Dedicated to Good and Ill Fortune, the temple was, he says, ornamented to the highest degree:

> Its intercolumnations, capitals, architraves, pediments, and basins, carved in Parian marble and in stone from the remotest mountains of India and Arabia, were all wonderful in number, size, and workmanship. Its vases, candelabra, tripods, cauldrons, and other such

4 Interior of Scrovegni Chapel, Padua, decorated by Giotto, *c.* 1305.

articles set out for sacrifices, were likewise numerous
and beautiful, and splendidly adorned with gold and
gems.

However, it is not the building itself on which Alberti lavishes
the most attention but rather a series of fictional paintings
on the walls inside.

The temple was, he explains, adorned with representations of female personifications, ten on either side to the left
and right, with each one relating directly to its opposite number. On the left, a series of figures embodying negative qualities
and moral vices included Envy, identified as the mother of
all the rest, along with Calumny, Indignation, Enmity and
others. On the right, Modesty was shown to be the mother of
a group of positive personifications including Peace of Mind,
Cultivation of Virtue and Praise. The attitudes and attributes
of all of the figures are described in turn, with each constitut-
ing an elaborate visual allegory. Thus Envy 'was depicted as a
decrepit and hunch-backed crone with a pallid face, bleary
eyes, and thick brows. She straddles a ten-foot rule, which
she holds with one hand, like a boy riding a hobby horse, while
in the other she holds a plumb-line. On her neck, she carries
a savage ape who tears her hair, cheeks, and ears with his
nails and teeth.' Modesty, on the other hand, was 'a beautiful
woman in a Coan garment [made from silk from the island
of Kos], her hair skilfully braided and wondrously arranged.
With one hand she presses her mouth, while with the other,
she clutches her robe to her thigh, wrapping her private parts
in its folds, and gazes at her bosom with pensive and down-
cast eyes.'[1]

Although Alberti is careful to locate his fictional temple
in a remote time and place, there is much about it that contemporaries would have found familiar. While he attended
Barzizza's school in Padua, he would have had the opportunity
to visit the large chapel built by the financier Enrico Scrovegni.
The chapel was famous for its frescoes, which had been completed by the Florentine painter Giotto and his workshop
around a century before Alberti was born (illus. 4). An image
of the Last Judgement covered the entrance wall, while the
long side walls were adorned with scenes from the lives of the
Virgin Mary and Christ. Beneath these, the painters represented a series of figures personifying moral virtues on the
right and vices on the left, each one corresponding to its
opposite number, so that, for example, Justice (illus. 5) sits
opposite Injustice (illus. 6). These figures were themselves
stationed between skilfully feigned faux marble panels that
made it seem as though exotic stones had been brought from
far-flung quarries to decorate the chapel. Many of the elements
of Alberti's gymnosophistic temple, in other words, could be
found there.

The battle between virtues and vices, or *psychomachia*, was
a favourite theme of medieval writers. In art, a related icono-
graphical tradition, in which virtues and vices were made to
square up to each other in a didactic moral stand-off, was
also widely employed. Giotto's personifications were just
one example among many. Alberti's description of the temple in *Paintings* suggests that he was receptive to this kind of
imagery. Discussion of the good stands at the heart of many
of his writings and he recognized that images, too, could be
the repositories of philosophical truth; that moral themes

could be the subject of visual as well as verbal reasoning. He may also have been thinking, in the *Paintings*, of techniques for the training of what was known as 'artificial memory', in which a person could learn to remember long sequences by constructing a mental building, or memory palace, and placing within it striking figures associated with words, things or ideas.

5 Giotto, *Justice*, c. 1305, Scrovegni Chapel, Padua.

The practice derived from the techniques of ancient orators, and its most extensive exposition occurred in a rhetorical handbook that Alberti knew well, the pseudo-Ciceronian *Rhetorica ad Herennium*.[2] These techniques of artificial memory were widely diffused and reiterated in the Middle Ages, and their principles may have influenced the production of schemes

6 Giotto, *Injustice*, c. 1305, Scrovegni Chapel, Padua.

such as Giotto's virtues and vices in the Scrovegni Chapel, which acted as reminders of the paths leading to heaven and hell. The artificial memory also suggested how meaning could reside in a fluid mental back and forth between images, places, words and things, something that itself points towards what we might term a broader hermeneutic preoccupation running through all of Alberti's work. His literary production, as a whole, shows him to have been deeply concerned with the entire realm of meaning, be it verbal, numerical or visual; and visual meaning was all around him.

Alberti inhabited an intensely pictorial world, populated by a dazzling array of images that were often undertaking important work: teaching, admonishing, telling stories and representing abstract ideas, as well as seeking to improve and sometimes to delight their beholders. In Venice, where he spent his early childhood, he would have seen the vast, Byzantine-style mosaics of San Marco (illus. 8), as well as the basilica's great altarpiece, the Pala d'Oro, encrusted with

7 Interior of the Palazzo della Ragione, Padua, 1920s.
8 Ceiling of San Marco's Basilica, Venice.

enamel icons, many of which came from Constantinople. In Padua the Scrovegni Chapel provided a masterclass in narrative painting, while allegories abounded in the city's civic chamber, the Palazzo della Ragione (illus. 7). Modern relief sculptures could be inspected in Bologna, in Jacopo della Quercia's Porta Magna for San Petronio, and ancient ones in Rome. There, within the space of an hour, a pedestrian could take in mosaics ranging from the early Christian to the late medieval periods (illus. 9), elaborate carvings on Roman triumphal arches (illus. 10), and cutting-edge contemporary Florentine fresco paintings such as those made by Masaccio and Masolino in the Basilica of San Clemente (illus. 11). A very broad array of pictorial art – icons, mosaics, panel paintings, frescoes showing narratives and allegories, relief sculptures, manuscript illuminations and so on – dating from antiquity to the present, produced in both pagan and Christian contexts,

9 Mosaics in the Basilica dei Santi Cosma e Damiano, Rome, 6th century.

and performing a wide variety of functions, was thus available for inspection in many of the cities in which Alberti had made his home.

The humanists were not insensitive to this abundance of visual meaning. They often employed visual metaphors and verbal images within their texts, and they habitually drew parallels between painting and writing. Sometimes they even discussed the works of individual artists. Preoccupied as they were with language, however, they did not deal in any systematic or substantial way with the visual arts. In *De commodis*, there are already hints of Alberti's desire for a deeper engagement, as well as a growing frustration at the constraints imposed by traditional scholarly practices. Thus he complains that if, as a scholar, 'you enquire into technical knowledge or painting or three-dimensional design, the academic disciplines will say: "This is the way you defraud *us* of your energies. From you we

10 Arch of Constantine, Rome, 313 CE. In addition to the Constantinian reliefs, the arch incorporates sculptures taken from monuments to Trajan, Hadrian and Marcus Aurelius.

will withhold knowledge of the highest things!'"[3] Neglect your literary studies even for a moment, he seems to say (especially if it is to turn your attention to a mere 'mechanical art') and the punishment will be terrible. Nonetheless a few years later he would brush off the histrionic threats of the tyrannical

11 Masaccio and Masolino, *St Catherine Disputing with the Philosophers* (Scenes from the Life of St Catherine of Alexandria), *c.* 1425–31, fresco, Castiglione Chapel, San Clemente, Rome.

disciplines and write a treatise on painting, making the extraordinary claim to speak not as a scholar but as a painter himself.

ON PAINTING

On Painting (*De pictura*) is a short but dense treatise that exists in both Latin and vernacular versions. Modern scholars had for many years assumed that the Latin text came first and that Alberti subsequently translated it in order to make it available to artists who were not literate in the ancient language. It has been demonstrated, however, that things probably happened the other way around.[4] As we saw in the first chapter, Alberti recorded that he completed his treatise in Florence at a quarter to nine on the evening of 26 August 1435. This was most likely the vernacular text. The Latin version is in several respects more elaborate. It might thus be that the vernacular served as a first draft for the Latin, or it could be that each was produced with a different audience in mind. In both versions the treatise is divided into three books. The first sets out some fundamental principles relating to geometry and optics, and ends with an account of what we now call perspective. The second examines the constituent parts of painting and considers how they might be combined into a composition. The third explores the character of the painter and the approach that he ought to take to his work, as well as some broader conceptual issues such as the relationship between painting and literature and the nature of beauty.

All this has the appearance of a systematic and methodical treatment of the subject. Yet this should not distract from the fundamental strangeness of Alberti's project. That strangeness begins with his authorial self-positioning. Alberti stresses throughout that he writes as a painter, and while we might take him at his word and assume that he did paint, he was of course not a professional painter but a writer. Those who painted for a living started out as young apprentices and worked their way up the hierarchy of a *bottega*, or workshop. While Alberti was chanting his Latin declensions with Barzizza, young painters would have been performing all manner of menial tasks, ranging from debt collection to grinding pigments, taking whatever opportunity they could to study their master's drawings and gradually improving their own skills. While Alberti studied law at university, painters of his age might have been matriculating into a guild, allowing them to set up as independent masters. Painters did not learn advanced Latin or conduct sophisticated analyses of the most recently rediscovered ancient texts, any more than humanists were taught how to erect the scaffolding necessary to fresco a chapel.

Corresponding to these differences in training was a difference in class. Alberti came from an old family of the Florentine elite: people who did not make paintings but commissioned them. When he arrived in Florence, he could have seen, in the sacristy of San Miniato, the frescoes that his grandfather Benedetto had ordered from the artist Spinello Aretino, illustrating the life of his name saint, St Benedict (illus. 12). Outside of the city, he might have visited the Oratory of Santa Caterina delle Ruote, where the same artist had painted scenes of the life of St Catherine for the Alberti (illus. 13). In both cases, Benedetto, already in exile and about

12 Spinello Aretino, frescoes showing the life of St Benedict, 1388, sacristy of the Basilica di San Miniato al Monte, Florence.

to depart for the Holy Land, had made specific provision in his will for the works to be completed. At Santa Croce, one of the city's largest and most prestigious basilicas, Alberti would have seen, in the main chapel, the stunning cycle of frescoes that his family had commissioned from Agnolo Gaddi, showing the legend of the True Cross (illus. 14). In every case, the family's coat of arms appeared prominently alongside the religious scenes (illus. 15).

The Alberti, then, were patrons, not painters. This would not be so remarkable had Alberti addressed himself solely and unambiguously to other humanists or to noblemen who might want to try their hand at painting, or even just know how to speak about it knowledgeably. These must have been the intended readership of the Latin version, and the dedicatory preface to that text in fact confirms this to be the case. But he also insists that his treatise is for *painters*, and it may well be that he produced the Tuscan version in the genuine hope that professional painters would read it. If so, then his project was a radical one indeed, attempting to foster an entirely new kind of meeting between theory and practice. Similarly remarkable is the fact that Alberti does not base his discussion on an empirical analysis of the painted works that were everywhere around him. After all, he was writing in Florence, in the midst of one of the most vigorous phases of the Renaissance. When he arrived there, Donatello and Luca della Robbia were at work on the marble singing galleries for the cathedral (illus. 16), Ghiberti was fashioning his second set of bronze doors for the Baptistery (illus. 17) and Masaccio and Masolino's frescoes in the Brancacci Chapel were less than a decade old. While he mentions some of the city's leading

13 Spinello Aretino, frescoes showing the life of St Catherine of Alexandria, c. 1388, Oratorio di Santa Caterina delle Ruote, Ponte a Ema.

14 Main chapel with frescoes of the *Legend of the True Cross* by Agnolo Gaddi, 1385–7, Basilica di Santa Croce, Florence.

artists in his letter to Brunelleschi, in the treatise itself he does not engage with this context at all. In fact, the only 'modern' work that he discusses is a mosaic in Rome by Giotto that was already well over a hundred years old. Instead, he aims to start from first principles, founding his discourse on his own experience as a painter, with frequent recourse to the twin authorities of nature and antiquity. The latter provides the vast majority of his examples of actual works of art – works that, in most cases, he had read about but not seen.

In this way, Alberti demonstrated his desire not to describe what painting was in fact, but to set it out in theory. He was keen to show that painting truly depended upon art (*ars*), or what the Greeks had called *techne*, a procedure that operates according to logical principles and that is therefore open to rational explanation. This led him to insist, at several points in the treatise, that a painter lacking in theoretical understanding could never produce something genuinely good.

15 Detail of the ceiling vault of the Oratorio di Santa Caterina delle Ruote. Frescoed chains run up the full length of the ribs and meet at a ring in the centre, making the entire vault into an Alberti coat of arms.

Given his claim to be the first to set out the principles of painting in this way, the implication seems to be that most professional painters were deficient, and that he, Alberti, would explain to them their own art; an audacious position, to say the least.

If Florentine artists were bemused by a humanist intellectual, the bastard son of a prominent exile, trying to instruct them about painting, scholars would also have had cause for surprise. Assuming that the vernacular *De pictura* really was aimed at professional painters, it would have represented an unprecedented intellectual transgression. It took complex theoretical material that normally existed only in Latin texts and transposed it into the vernacular. In so doing, it sought to bring that material, which was usually the stuff of rarefied discussion in grammar schools and universities, into the artist's *bottega*. Lucia Bertolini has argued that, in writing the Tuscan text, Alberti envisaged a kind of painter who did

16 Luca della Robbia, Cantoria, *c.* 1431–8, marble, Museo dell'Opera del Duomo, Florence.

not yet exist and who would only come to do so in the next
generation with figures such as Piero della Francesca and
Leonardo da Vinci. According to this view, Alberti imagined
his reader as an artist who was willing to embrace theory and
to make it the foundation of his work, but who remained a
professional practitioner rather than a humanist.[5] Certainly,
some of Alberti's discourse was markedly technical in character, falling outside of the standard fare of humanist debate.
Thus he begins the first book of *De pictura* with some basic
principles of plane geometry, drawn from the *Elements* of
Euclid, a fundamental text dating from around 300 BCE. He
explains how points can be connected to make lines, which

17 Lorenzo Ghiberti, *Jacob and Esau*, 1425–52, gilded bronze panel from the
Baptistery doors (*Gates of Paradise*), Museo dell'Opera del Duomo, Florence.

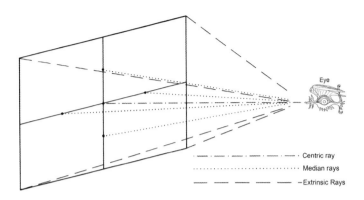

in turn can be joined at various angles to create surfaces, and adds that those surfaces will be flat, convex or concave, or some combination of any of those three.[6] He also draws on ancient and medieval optics to provide an account of how we see such surfaces, saying that sight is transmitted by way of visual rays that can be divided into three kinds: the extrinsic rays that strike the edges of the surface, the median rays that strike its interior, and the centric ray that hits dead centre at an angle of 90 degrees. Together they form a pyramid, the base of which corresponds to the object seen and the apex of which rests in the eye (illus. 18).[7]

In setting out these principles, Alberti walks a tightrope. He does not, he says, wish to speak as a mathematician but as a painter, relating only as much as it is necessary for the painter to know. Geometers, he asserts, examine figures in the mind with no regard for their physical being, while painters should concern themselves only with what is visible. For this reason, Alberti says at the outset that he must use a more embodied knowledge or 'più grassa Minerva' when dealing with this subject.[8] The reference here is to the Roman goddess of wisdom,

18 Diagram of visual pyramid. Drawing by Oliver Matthews, based on an illustration in Leon Battista Alberti, *On Painting*, trans. Cecil Grayson (London, 1991).

Minerva, and the term 'più grassa' – literally, fattier – might best be understood as 'more bodily', signalling that he will shy away from total abstraction and keep one eye trained on the physical world. As a result, he peppers his discourse with tangible analogies: outlines are described as hems or ribbons; a flat surface is likened to a clear pool of water, a concave one to the inside of an eggshell and a convex one to the exteriors of pipes and columns. At the same time, Alberti does not wish to underplay the difficult, mathematical nature of his discussion. At the end of the first book, when the most complicated issues have been broached, he asserts, starkly, that these matters cannot be understood by everybody, and that anybody who has not got it at the first reading probably never will.

PERSPECTIVE

A good example of such complicated issues is perspective. This is undoubtedly one of the most significant and also one of the most elusive ideas in the history of art. For some scholars today, it signals a Renaissance revolution in epistemology, an entirely novel way to conceive of space and a leap into a new paradigm of vision. For others it is merely a tool for painting – useful, but hardly a conceptual game-changer. Some argue that different forms of perspective have existed at different moments in history, while others use the term only to denote the set of practices that emerged from the fifteenth century onwards. Alberti himself does not use the word *prospettiva* at all. Instead he speaks of the *intersegazione* (intersection), since what he really describes is a technique for making an image that acts as an intersection of the visual pyramid – one that, owing to the Euclidian principle of similar triangles, will of necessity be proportional to the original image seen. The method, which Alberti says in the Latin version is his own, is set out step by step, though his language is far from clear and the passage is difficult to follow. Nonetheless, much of what it touches on is now familiar.

Most art history students will be conversant with some of the main elements of a one-point perspective construction: the horizon line (which Alberti calls the 'centric line'), vanishing point ('centric point'), orthogonals (for which he has no specific term) and transversals (*linee… transverse*). In the *De pictura* Alberti explains how all of these things may be arranged so as to create a grid that will produce a convincing illusion of a three-dimensional space. The whole thing will take its measure from the notional size of a figure within the painting, since Alberti says that he begins by drawing a rectangle of whatever size he likes and then deciding how tall a person standing at the front of the picture would be. He then takes the height of that figure and divides it into three, saying that each third should be considered equivalent to a *braccio*, a Florentine unit of measurement relating (more by convention than measure) to the length of an arm. Having established this unit of measure, he uses it to mark evenly spaced points along the baseline of his rectangle, each placed one '*braccio*' apart. He next places a point further up, but no higher than the head of the figure at the front. This he calls 'the centric point', since it is the place that the centric ray should strike, though today it is usually described as 'the vanishing point'. From this point, he draws what we would now call orthogonal lines (lines that are understood as being at right angles to the front of the picture, although that is not how they will appear to the eye) so that each one leads to a division on the baseline.

So far, so straightforward, but there is more to Alberti's method. In fact, the most important part of it concerns the transversal lines that run horizontally across the orthogonals. These have to be placed so that the distance between them gradually diminishes in a mathematically consistent manner. Alberti achieves this by introducing another point of view from the side. On a separate surface he draws a horizontal line and divides it in the same way as the baseline of the rectangle. At one end of the line, he places a point at the height of the centric point. From there he draws further lines to the divisions below. He then cuts those lines with a perpendicular one, which he places at a point that corresponds with whatever he considers to be the ideal viewing distance from the painting. Where the vertical intersects with the diagonals, this indicates where the transversals should be placed in the painting. Once these have been drawn in, Alberti adds a final line: the centric line (or horizon), which runs straight through the centric point from one side of the rectangle to the other. This combination of views from front and side ultimately results in a kind of gridded or chequerboard

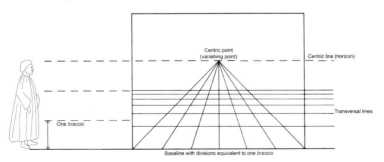

19 Diagram of perspective construction. Drawing by Oliver Matthews.

pavement that gives the impression of recession into depth
(illus. 19).

Alberti explains all of this on the level of practice. He does
not provide much theoretical explanation of *why* his method
works, only assuring us that it does. Of course, the really
important thing is what it allows you to do. With perspective,
the artist is able to produce, on a flat surface, a persuasive
image of a three-dimensional space. The relative sizes of
objects can then be determined depending on their distance
from the viewer, and this can be done in a consistent way, so
that the image is governed by a unitary spatial logic. Regular
objects can be shown to conform to this logic, which will determine the manner in which they appear to recede into depth.

To see how this works, just look, for example, at Benozzo
Gozzoli's fresco in the hilltown of San Gimignano, which

20 Benozzo Gozzoli, *The School of Tagaste*, 1464–5, fresco, main chapel of the
Convento di Sant'Agostino, San Gimignano.

represents the schooldays of the young St Augustine (illus. 20).
In a scene showing the School of Tagaste, we see Augustine,
on the left, greeted by the schoolmaster; on the right we see
him engrossed in his studies, while another boy is punished.
All of this takes place within an urban setting of considerable
complexity. The chequered pavements upon which the figures
stand are made up of transversals and orthogonals, the angles
and positioning of which are all determined by the underlying
perspective grid. The same is true of the coffers (the grid
pattern) on the ceiling of the structure on the left. Were we
to follow all of these orthogonal lines, we would find that they
meet at a single point – the centric or 'vanishing' point – just
above the head of the central child in yellow. This is not only
true of the lines on the floors and the ceilings, however. Every
orthogonal in the composition leads there, including those that
define the side faces of the buildings. Thus all of the architectural structures diminish as they move further from us, and
the figures placed among them also decrease in size. Look at
the head of the woman in bluish green who stands in the
middle ground. It is placed around the same height as the eyes
of the child in front (Alberti observes that the heads of people
seen at various distances will generally appear at around the
same level) but her feet, which are positioned on a higher
transversal of the grid, do not even reach his elbow. Because
of the perspectival system, however, we do not see her as a
miniature sprite hovering by the boy's shoulder. Instead, we
readily understand that she is a fully grown adult standing
further away. All of this produces such a compelling sense of
place that we feel we could almost step into this city, round
its corners, and explore its streets and alleyways.

A long art-historical tradition considers Brunelleschi – the architect of the dome of Florence cathedral – to have invented perspective, and holds that Alberti merely wrote down the method. Undoubtedly, Brunelleschi did work on systems for the rendering of mathematically realized images of three-dimensional spaces on flat surfaces. How similar his methods were to those later described by Alberti is not entirely clear, but from what we know of them they would seem to be quite different. It is also true that artists produced paintings according to techniques that are similar, though not identical, to Alberti's system, some years before he wrote the *De pictura*. Masaccio's painting of the *Holy Trinity* in the church of Santa Maria Novella in Florence is often cited in this regard (illus. 21). We might thus conclude that Alberti was one of a number of people in the period working on perspectival techniques; he was, however, the first to produce a formalized, written account of his method intended for general application.[9] In so doing he initiated a theoretical discourse that would be taken up by artist-intellectuals of the following generation such as Piero della Francesca and Leonardo da Vinci and elaborated on throughout the Renaissance and beyond.

NARRATIVE

Of course, this type of geometrical-mathematical discourse will only take an artist so far. Alberti combined it, in the first book of his treatise, with a basic explanation of how we see colours. Taken as a whole, this was intended to provide the practitioners with the necessary rudiments of theory, paving the way for him to turn, in the next book, to painting itself.

21 Masaccio, *Holy Trinity*, c. 1425–8, fresco, Santa Maria Novella, Florence.

He begins by extolling painting's virtues and calling it the mistress of all the arts. It was, he claims, an important part of ancient Greek education, admired by ancient philosophers and emperors. The painter has the power to make the absent present and to represent the dead to the living, and it is little wonder that such a man should find himself revered 'almost as a second god'.[10] Although he cites a number of historical examples, Alberti states that he will not, like the ancient writer Pliny the Elder, provide a history of painting. Rather, his intention is 'to build an art of painting, *ex novo*': to produce, that is, a written, theoretical account based on first principles.[11] With this in mind, he proceeds with his explanation, starting by dividing painting into three parts: circumscription, composition and the reception of lights.

Circumscription denotes the process of outlining. The painter should use very fine, almost invisible lines, and should aim for precision. In order to achieve this exactitude, Alberti recommends the use of a device: a fine gauze veil with a regular grid of threads woven into it, stretched across a wooden frame. Looking through the veil, the painter can apprehend what he sees as a series of parts and plot the location of each one of them. This will assist with the accurate representation of three-dimensional objects, the outlines of which will vary according to their position relative to the beholder. As anybody who has attempted to draw will know, foreshortening, the phenomenon by which an object appears truncated when it projects towards us, is especially difficult to capture, and the veil is presumably designed to help with this. At the same time, it will assist with the representation of irregular forms that cannot easily be mapped onto the perspective grid. Such is the power of this device that Alberti wonders how anybody could draw effectively without it.[12]

The concern with the accurate rendering of three-dimensional forms also informs his discussion of the third part of painting, the reception of lights. The painter ought to have an excellent understanding of light and shade in order to show objects in maximum relief, for this is the thing that 'the artist must above all desire'.[13] He should pay attention to the play of light on different surfaces, using white and black to modulate his colours while avoiding the use of either of them on its own. Alberti discusses which colours will sit happily together, and warns against the use of gold leaf, a prominent feature of medieval altarpieces and an element that still appeared in many of the most prestigious works of art produced in his own day. Whenever he went to visit the tombs of his grandfather Benedetto and his other ancestors in the friars' choir at Santa Croce, he would have seen both the great gilded altarpiece made by Ugolino di Nerio for the high altar there and the many shining touches of metal leaf in the surrounding frescoes of the legend of the True Cross, one of the last great commissions undertaken by the Alberti family before their expulsion from the city. Nonetheless, Alberti seems to have considered the application of such metals to be an abrogation of the artist's responsibility to represent all things with paint. Perhaps he also viewed them as archaic.

In between circumscription and reception of lights, he turns to composition. This discussion stands at the centre of both Book Two and the entire treatise. 'Composition', he says, 'is that procedure in painting whereby the parts are composed together in a picture. The great work of the painter is the *istoria* [*historia* in the Latin version].'[14] By this, broadly speaking, he means a narrative.[15] The (*h*)*istoria* might relate to religious history, showing an episode from the Bible or the life of a saint (as in the Gozzoli example above). It could represent a scene from ancient mythology or it might illustrate an episode recounted by ancient historians. Alberti also seems to include some allegorical paintings – paintings in which a group of people stands for an idea. In every case, there must be figures performing an action. This might seem very broad, but it excludes a lot of the art of Alberti's own day: paintings of single figures, for a start. Depictions of individual saints, and of the Virgin Mary with the Christ child, abounded in Italian churches. Sometimes these could be very large and imposing, but Alberti declares that 'the great work of the painter is not a colossus but an *istoria*.'[16] Images of saints   whether alone or in groups – were often made for devotional purposes, serving as aids to meditation. Such paintings were more numerous than the narratives that Alberti prized. Why, then, this focus on the *istoria*?

The answer takes us back to meaning. The *istoria* is above all an intelligible image, capable of conveying significant ideas about human beings and the actions they perform – and those things were the raw materials of the moral philosophy with which Alberti was so concerned. That intelligibility was founded upon a rational structuring, which Alberti explained by invoking another hierarchy: 'parts of the *istoria* are the bodies, part of the body is the member, and part of the member is the surface.'[17] So, the surfaces described in the first book, built from points, lines and angles, can be combined to make limbs and body-parts, which can in turn be amalgamated into bodies that together will perform the action that constitutes the *istoria*. This is the job of composition, and it is no simple task. If the bodies are to function properly, their constituent parts must all conform in size and type. There can be no plump-faced man with emaciated arms, no young maiden with old, roughened hands, and no figure with members that are out of scale to each other.[18] In the body, then, as in the entire painting, proportion must reign, and Alberti invokes another sequence to explain how it might be achieved. When painting living creatures, he says, it is best 'first to sketch in the bones, for as they bend very little indeed, they always occupy a certain determined position. Then add the sinews and muscles, and finally clothe the bones and muscles with flesh and skin.'[19] These bodies should then be put to work to make images that are both rationally and emotionally powerful. How is this to be achieved?

'An *istoria*', Alberti observes, 'will move spectators when the men painted in the picture outwardly demonstrate their own feelings as clearly as possible. Nature provides – and there is nothing to be found more rapacious of her like than she – that we mourn with the mourners, laugh with those who laugh, and grieve with the grief stricken. Yet these feelings are known from movements of the body.'[20] Emotions such as melancholy, anger and joy will all find expression in an individual's physical bearing. Thus Alberti devotes considerable attention to movement, gesture and posture; those things that make up what is today known as 'body language'. The term is an apt one, because language was not far from his mind. As Michael Baxandall has shown, Alberti seems to have based his theory of composition on ancient accounts of rhetoric, in which 'composition' denoted the progression, within a periodic sentence, from word to phrase, to clause, to sentence. This sequence, which would have been familiar to anybody with rhetorical training, is mirrored in Alberti's own hierarchy of surface, member, body, *istoria*.[21] This might suggest that he viewed painting as a form of visual eloquence, capable of working on our emotions and thoughts – particularly since, as Baxandall demonstrates, other aspects of Alberti's theory also correspond with rhetorical concerns. For example, Alberti approves of both variety and abundance, but says that each of them must be strictly limited. This implies disapproval of some fifteenth-century painting in which copiousness and diversity seem to be ends in themselves but it could equally apply to forms of rhetoric judged to lack a sufficiently rigorous structure.[22]

All of this does not, however, signal that *De pictura* is at heart only a humanist performance, in which painting is reduced to language and a dry, scholarly apparatus is interposed between the viewer and the artwork. In reality, Alberti approaches painting with the instruments at his disposal. Rhetorical treatises such as Quintilian's *Institutio oratoria* constituted the only fairly complete descriptions of any art to survive from antiquity, and thus offered a particularly powerful model.[23] Alberti's intellectual apparatus would undoubtedly have attracted the interest of humanist readers of the Latin text, but it would not have been so visible to the artisans that he seems to have intended as the readership of the original vernacular version (figures such as Brunelleschi). In fact, Alberti emphasizes that painting 'alone is equally pleasing to both learned and unlearned; and it rarely happens in any other art that what pleases the knowledgeable also attracts the ignorant'.[24] He might have wanted painters to acquire some learning in order to make good works, but he did not suggest that any was required in order to appreciate them. And while we might suspect that Alberti's account of painting is altogether too verbal and insufficiently visual, we should note his claims that a good composition will achieve not only clarity but beauty – an intensely visual goal if ever there was one.

In setting out these positions, Alberti uses many ancient sources, but his chief example is a medieval rather than an ancient work. Giotto's celebrated mosaic of the *Navicella* was situated in St Peter's Basilica in Rome. It was severely damaged in the seventeenth century during the rebuilding of the church, but Alberti would have had ample opportunity to study it in its original form (illus. 22 and 23). It shows the moment when, caught in a terrible storm, the disciples saw Jesus walking towards them across the water. When Peter asked if he could go out to him, Jesus summoned him, but

22 Giotto, *Navicella*, 1305–13, mosaic, St Peter's Basilica, Vatican City. Large sections of the mosaic have been remade and it has been reaffixed in its present situation following the rebuilding of the basilica.

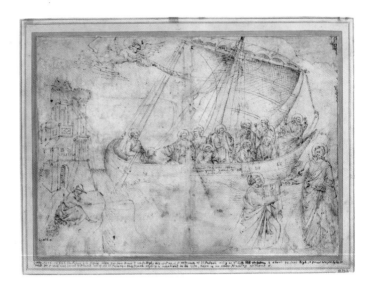

Peter soon began to sink. Hauling him out of the waves, Jesus delivered to Peter the famous reproach 'O thou of little faith,' before they both returned to the boat and the storm was calmed (Matthew 14:24–32). In this mosaic, Alberti found much of what he sought: a limited number of figures whose varied gestures and bodily attitudes served to convey a narrative that was both legible and emotionally compelling. Thus he says:

> they praise the boat painted in Rome, in which our own Tuscan painter Giotto placed eleven disciples, all of them moved by fear upon seeing one of their companions walk upon the water, each showing such clear signs of his agitation in his face and entire body that their individual emotions are discernible in every one of them.[25]

23 Parri Spinelli, free copy of Giotto's *Navicella*, showing the composition before it was remade, *c.* 1420, pen and brown ink.

PARTS AND WHOLES

This one, prominent citation of Giotto helps us to envision
what an Albertian *istoria* might look like, but it also draws
attention to the temporal uncertainty that pervades Alberti's
treatise. In some ways *De pictura* seems to be a project entirely
of the present, aimed at influencing its own time. The letter
to Brunelleschi certainly suggests that Alberti saw it as connected to contemporary practice. Yet contemporary art is
absent from the treatise while a late medieval mosaic – a
kind of modern classic by that time – makes a pivotal
appearance. Ancient works are mentioned frequently but
the authority of antiquity is limited in *De pictura*, and it is not
clear whether Alberti believed that the ancients possessed
the most important part of painting: composition. Judging
by their surviving works, he observes, they did not (assuming
that he includes them when he refers to *maiores nostros*: 'our
ancestors').[26] His theory is in some ways profoundly classical,
but the simple revival of antiquity is not Alberti's project.
Rather, his classicism finds voice in his commitment to the
whole; his insistence that every part must work towards a
single end and that all superfluity must be omitted. This can
be detected in his praise of the *Navicella*, where he observes
that the *entire* body of *every* disciple conveys the requisite
emotion. 'In every painting,' he says, 'the principle should be
observed that all the members should fulfil their function
according to the action performed, in such a way that not
even the smallest limb fails to play its appropriate part.'[27]
Moving from members to bodies, he advises that 'everything
the people in the painting do among themselves, or perform

in relation to the spectators, must fit together to represent and explain the *istoria*.'[28]

This preoccupation with the complete work, in which every part plays its role and nothing without a role may be included, can be found within a wide range of what might broadly be termed 'classical' thinking about art. Alberti would have encountered it in ancient philosophy and poetics, and, as we will see in Chapter Eight, he also discovered it in architecture. Having assimilated this concern, he made it into a key component of his own hermeneutic project and placed it at the centre of his theory of literary and pictorial meaning.

In this regard we might think back to the analogy of the mosaic in the *Profugiorum*, where composition is also a central issue. The makers of the temple of Diana are said to have composed pictures ('compose quella e quell'altra pittura'), Agnolo's style is described as composed ('composto') and a well-wrought 'literary mosaic' like Agnolo's speech is praised as a 'most composed work' ('compositissima opera'). And just like the *istoria*, the best literary mosaic will form a whole in which 'many and various things are made one' and in which 'everything corresponds to one tone, everything partakes equally of one plan, everything follows one line, everything conforms to one design'.[29] Yet this is only part of the story. Alberti was also intensely aware of cultural disjunction: the fragmentation caused by the collapse of the ancient world. Such awareness was implicit in the humanist project, and it is no coincidence that Petrarch, a pioneer of humanist thought, was a key figure in the development of the notion of the 'fragment' in its modern sense. In the mosaic simile, which evokes the practice of architectural spoliation, we discover

an important tension, for Alberti alludes to the power of
disaggregation even as he outlines an aesthetic theory based
around the whole. That is to say, his vision of a timeless, complete and fully intelligible order is forced to cohabit with his
consciousness of ubiquitous partiality and historical contingency. Thus intelligibility is achieved in the mosaic, yet in the
same moment meaning threatens to unmake itself. This tension runs throughout Alberti's texts concerning literature and
visual art. It might also be connected with the theme of exile,
a constant in his writing and something that is prominent in
the letter to Brunelleschi, in which the notion of return is
forced to coexist with anxiety about the impossibility of recuperation. The exile's return can itself be understood as an
attempt at making whole and restoring meaning. In Alberti's
case, however, any such attempt was fraught with difficulty.

Speaking more broadly, a marked concern with centres and
margins can be found in Alberti's aesthetic theories and, by
extension, in all of his thought. With its centric ray, centric line
and centric point, *De pictura* seems to treat the centre as a kind
of anchor of meaning. Alberti, as we have seen, had grown up
within a highly centralized spatial hierarchy. His life began on
the margins of that hierarchy, but by the time he wrote the
De pictura he had finally reached the centre. There he might
have expected to encounter wholeness and meaning. On the
other hand, Alberti was also conscious of the importance of
point of view – another key preoccupation of his treatise
on painting – and he knew that viewing had to take place at
a determined distance.

The idea is implicit in the simile of the mosaic in the
Profugiorum. While the topos of a 'mosaic of speech' goes back

to several antique sources, Alberti may have been thinking specifically of the treatise *On Order* by St Augustine – the man whose childhood was depicted in Gozzoli's fresco.[30] In Augustine's treatise the mosaic stands for the entire order of the universe. Speaking of those who deny the existence of a divine ordering, the saint says:

> The situation is akin to that of one who, confined to surveying a single section of a mosaic floor, looked at it too closely, and then blamed the artisan for being ignorant of order and composition. In reality it is he himself who, in concentrating on an apparently disordered variety of small coloured cubes, failed to notice the larger mosaic work. The apparent disorder of the elements really comes together in the unity of a beautiful portrait.[31]

To see properly, in other words, one must stand back. Such distancing is key to Alberti's thinking: in his notion of perspective; in the atemporal untimeliness that makes him neither ancient nor modern; and in his self-positioning as an exile-author. In this sense, he continually moves back and forth between imaginative centres and margins, placing himself at the heart of cultural debates while also claiming the status of an outsider. Alberti, we might say, alternately steps through the window to become an actor in the *istoria* and stands outside of it, looking in. In the chapters that follow, we will observe this process further as he turns his mind to key elements of his social world: the individual, the family and the city.

FOUR

The Self

By the middle of the century Alberti was building temples not only in words but in stone. Probably sometime between 1450 and 1454 he began the process of redesigning the exterior of the church of San Francesco in the eastern coastal city of Rimini. His journey from humanist writer to designer of buildings was not so much rare as unique. Quite how he undertook it is a complicated question. No documents remain that indicate the circumstances under which he became involved in the project at Rimini. There is no record of him visiting the city (although he must surely have done so) and it seems that, for the most part, he supervised construction from Rome. Nonetheless, the documentary record shows clearly that Alberti was responsible for the design, that he produced drawings and a model, that the leading masons on the project felt it necessary to travel to Rome to consult him, that he was held in high esteem, and that his judgement was considered authoritative. In other words, he occupied a position that we would normally describe as 'architect'.

If this was Alberti's first architectural work, it was an ambitious one. San Francesco was a large, gothic basilica constructed in the thirteenth and fourteenth centuries (and recently remodelled, with the addition of new side chapels). Alberti's scheme was to transform it entirely, wrapping the outside in a new exoskeleton and skin. A medal that includes an image of the building indicates that he planned a large dome over the east end, something that represented a significant engineering challenge (illus. 24). An apse was also probably envisaged, though it was never constructed, and some believe that Alberti must also have intended to make a transept, though the matter is disputed.[1] A facade of white Istrian stone was only partially completed, with the central, upper arch shown on the medal left unfinished and the decoration on the curved spandrels on either side (which Alberti later changed to make them straight) never applied.

Below, the facade was articulated by round arches and columns, while the entrance portal was richly decorated with inlaid purple porphyry and green serpentine (illus. 25). The arches and columns are derived from Roman architecture, including Rimini's own most important ancient structure, the Arch of Augustus, as well as triumphal arches in Rome

24 Unknown artist, after Matteo de' Pasti, medal showing the Tempio Malatestiano, Rimini, c. 1454, bronze.

such as the Arch of Constantine, which provided a model for
the tripartite division of the facade, and the entablature that
projects above the columns (see illus. 10 and 26). The coloured
stones were taken from late antique buildings in nearby
Ravenna, the complex revetments of which were no doubt a
major influence. As has recently been pointed out, the inlaid
ovals, set both vertically and horizontally, are an erudite quotation from St Mark's basilica in Venice, a building that Alberti
studied closely and that also perhaps inspired aspects of the
never-completed upper section.[2] To contemporary observers,
this extraordinary ensemble must have seemed like nothing
so much as an ancient temple – a designation that appears
on the medal and that would have made sense to Alberti, who
habitually used the word 'temple' to refer to churches. It is
perhaps not surprising then that over time it has become

25 Tempio Malatestiano (San Francesco), Rimini, new facade begun *c.* 1453.

26 Arch of Augustus, Rimini, 27 BCE.

27 Tempio Malatestiano under construction, in Basinio de' Basini of Parma, *Hesperis* (1455).

commonplace not to refer to the building as San Francesco but rather as the Tempio Malatestiano, or Malatestan Temple (illus. 27).

The adjective 'Malatestiano' refers to Sigismondo Malatesta, the lord of Rimini. As the patron of the work, it was he who ordered and paid for the rebuilding and he who had ultimate authority. The project had started in 1447 with the reshaping of one chapel and the construction of another. It then expanded to encompass the remodelling of the entire interior, before growing further still to include the exterior works. Some scholars believe that Alberti contributed to the decoration of the interior, but others confine his involvement to the exterior only. An inscription on the church says that Sigismondo undertook the renovation on account of a vow, something that is affirmed on the medal, which bears the date of 1450, referring not to its own facture but to the time when the vow was made. Sigismondo was a *condottiere*, or commander of a mercenary army, who had risen to the lordship of Rimini at the age of seventeen, following the death of his brother Galeotto. There he presided over a humanist court culture marked by intense admiration of antiquity, and ancient Greece in particular. His poets hymned him as a new Odysseus, a warrior hero for his time. He in turn honoured the intellectuals of his court by providing them with magnificent tombs, arrayed along the flank of his new temple, set under great round arches and separated by piers whose design is inspired by the Colosseum in Rome (illus. 28).[3] Known as an ardent lover of women and a skilful and daring player in the great game of Italian politics, the lord of Rimini was a larger than life, if morally compromised, figure.[4]

Sigismondo enjoyed a meteoric rise but he also underwent a dramatic fall. It came about through the enmity of Pope Pius II, who became increasingly frustrated with what he regarded as the disloyalty and the unwarranted territorial expansion of an upstart ruler who, as a papal vicar, was supposed to owe him obedience. His anger grew to such a degree that in 1460 the pope not only excommunicated Sigismondo but subjected him to the only reverse canonization in history, inverting the process whereby somebody was made a saint and instead declaring the lord of Rimini to be a citizen of hell.[5] As part of this process, Pius had Sigismondo's effigy burned (three times!) in Rome and also published a lengthy screed in which he accused his adversary of a litany of crimes: murder, fratricide, rape, sodomy and necrophilia, to name just a few. He decried the Tempio as a pagan monstrosity built by Sigismondo to deify his mistress (and eventual wife) Isotta

28 Tombs in the side arches of the Tempio Malatestiano.

degli Atti. The accusations were histrionic but effective. Little by little, power drained from the lord of Rimini. Finally defeated by his rival *condottiere* Federico da Montefeltro of Urbino, he died a prisoner in Rome in 1468, leaving his great temple unfinished. Quite what Pius thought about the involvement of his scribe in the design is not known. It is notable, however, that the pope's characterization of Sigismondo, in his *Commentaries*, as an expert in simulation and dissimulation and an individual who was able swiftly to master all manner of activities, is curiously close to contemporaneous accounts of Alberti.[6]

For Jacob Burckhardt, writing in the nineteenth century, Sigismondo was an example – albeit an ambivalent one – of what he termed the Renaissance 'individual': a figure who relied on his own talents and virtues and who eschewed the type of communal and corporate identities that the Swiss historian associated with the Middle Ages. However, it was Alberti – the 'universal man' – that Burckhardt considered to be the real Renaissance individual par excellence. This notion of Renaissance individualism no longer receives much credence from historians, but it has to some extent persisted by way of a different but related concept that has continued to exert a profound influence on discussions of Alberti: the self.

We have already encountered some of the ways in which Alberti seems to approach the idea in his writings. The complex authorial positioning that accompanied the *Philodoxeos fabula*, the reflection upon his own activity as a scholar in *De commodis* and the consideration of his 'return' from exile in the letter to Brunelleschi all point towards it. We have seen Alberti appear as a character in his own dialogue, the *Profugiorum ab erumna*, standing by as the other participants discuss his literary method. In *De pictura* his presence is everywhere. Not only does he speak directly, in his own voice, but he posits himself as the only true origin of his discourse. Thus when he begins his explanation of perspective – a crucial moment in the history of art if ever there were one – he presents it as being spun entirely from his own self, writing: 'let me tell you what I do when I am painting. First of all, on the surface on which I am going to paint, I draw a rectangle of whatever size I want, which I regard as an open window through which the subject to be painted is seen; and I decide how large I wish the human figures in the painting to be.'[7] There is a marked foregrounding of individual will here; the method is Alberti's and it is upon his initial arbitration that the entire structure of any resulting *istoria* will rest: I do, I want, I decide.

That painting could have particular implications for the consideration of the self is perhaps signalled towards the start of Book II, when Alberti suggests that its inventor might have been Narcissus. Expanding on the importance of painting for all of the arts, he says: 'consequently I used to tell my friends that the inventor of painting, according to the poets, was Narcissus, who was turned into a flower; for, as painting is the flower of all the arts, so the entire tale of Narcissus fits our purpose perfectly. What is painting but the act of embracing by means of art the surface of the pool?'[8] Of course, Alberti knew nothing of the Freudian theory of narcissism, and we cannot apply it to him retrospectively. His preoccupation with the self takes the form of intense engagement with a philosophical problem, not a psychological disorder. Yet the inclusion of Narcissus does alert us to the possibility that, for Alberti, reflexivity lies at the heart of painting, an art that he sees as deriving from the act of gazing upon one's own reflection. Although it is not likely that he adopted Brunelleschi's method, he may have known that the older man's first perspective demonstration had involved looking through a hole in the back of a painted panel and seeing the front of that panel reflected in a mirror. At the centre of the image, where Alberti would later place his centric point, viewers would thus have encountered their own eye – or, perhaps better, their own gaze. Perhaps some memory of this remained in Alberti's treatise, even if he did replace that eye with a point located 'almost at infinity'. Could it be, then, that a painting, made according to one's own will and judgement, was a site in which one might encounter oneself, already present as another, at a point somehow located both on the horizon and at the centre?

If so, then the encounter was surely an unstable one. As Alberti says, the *entire* Narcissus myth must be considered, and the myth is far from comforting.[9] Narcissus' quest to embrace the pool (or rather the image of himself on the pool's surface) was ultimately futile. It is not simply that he was unable to do it; it is something that *cannot* be done. This realization provides an important key for understanding Alberti's broader reflexivity. If the self was already somehow present in painting, it was no less evident in text. Alberti encountered himself time and again in his written works, but often in an oblique and fragmentary way. The self that he sought and repeatedly actualized was a precarious one. It carried the knowledge of its own precariousness inside of it, and it often announced that precariousness loudly, even as it aspired to fixity and groundedness. To see how, we might turn momentarily from painting and writing and consider the art of sculpture.

THE WRITER IN RELIEF

Alberti claimed to have been a practitioner of sculpture, and later in life he wrote a short treatise about it. There is no surviving sculptural work that can be attributed to him with complete certainty, but he is usually considered to be the maker of a bronze portrait plaque showing his own head in profile (illus. 29). Oval in shape, the plaque is surprisingly large at around 20 × 13.5 cm (8 × 5½ in.); in fact it is about the size of the book you are reading now. Pictured with a long, straight nose, his hair closely cropped and with drapery knotted

29 Leon Battista Alberti (attributed), *Self-portrait*, *c*. 1435, bronze.

beneath his neck, Alberti looks like an ancient Roman as he stares impassively towards the left. The portrait is usually (though not securely) dated to around 1435, and if this is correct then it would make it contemporary with the first version of *De pictura*, completed that same year. Alberti had undoubtedly been hugely impressed by Florentine art, and it is notable that all of the artists he refers to in the letter to

30 Leon Battista Alberti (?), winged eye and motto from a manuscript of *Della famiglia*, c. 1438, ink on paper.

Brunelleschi (assuming that Masaccio, as seems likely, refers to Maso di Bartolomeo, and not to the more famous painter who is now known by that name) were makers of sculptural reliefs.[10] The plaque, which reveals a certain amateurishness in the modelling and contains a noticeable flaw in the casting, does not seem to be the work of professionals such as these and might credibly be considered the creation of a gifted amateur. In any case, there can be no doubt about the subject, because his name is written in abbreviated form along the right-hand side: L BAP, standing for Leo Baptista.[11]

Baptista is simply the Latinized form of Battista, the name that he was given by his father. But Leo? This is a name that he gave himself, at least as early as 1433.[12] To name oneself in such a way was not a common act, and nor did he choose just any name. Leo, or Leon(e) in Italian, means 'lion', an animal often associated with royalty, strength, beauty and any number of other positive attributes. Alberti would himself go on to write animal fables in which lions appear in exactly this way. As we have seen, his first work had also involved a prominent act of naming when he adopted the false name – or, better, the pseudonym – of Lepidus, part of a complicated name-game that seems to betray an intense early interest in authorial identity. In giving himself the new name of Leo – as a 'true' name rather than a pseudonym, and one that was meant to be used in life as well as in literature – he advanced this project considerably. Not only did the name associate him with particular qualities (in a similar way to the characters' names in the comedy *Philodoxeos*) but it proclaimed a kind of twin paternity. He was Battista, the son of Lorenzo, but he was also Leo, the son of himself.

These are not the only markers of identity present on the plaque. On the left-hand side is a winged eye, tucked in between Alberti's chin and a large knot of drapery, whose form it rather echoes. It stares straight out at the viewer, with rays undulating from its corners. This winged eye is Alberti's personal image and device, adopted as a sign for himself and appearing in various places in both sculpted and graphic form (illus. 30). In its mobility, it seems to speak to his voracious desire for knowledge and his will to investigate many things. It embodies an almost semi-divine dynamism while also perhaps gesturing towards Alberti's peripatetic life as an exile-scholar. It must also surely relate to his new orientation towards the visual arts; his growing interest in the production of visual meaning, which finds such clear expression in *De pictura* of the same years. This eye, which looks directly at us, stands in stark contrast to the one in Alberti's head, which is seen in profile and presents itself as an object for our vision rather than a locus of subjectivity. It is a duality that might once again remind us of painting and the perspective system. For if we associate the vanishing point with an eye that stares out of the painting, straight along the centric ray, to meet the gaze of the beholder, then we should also remember the other gaze that was needed to produce the perspectival order: the view from the side that determines the placing of the transversals. On the plaque, it is as though these two views have been compressed into one, resulting in a strange and abbreviated allegory of pictorial reflexivity, captured within a thoroughly un-perspectival visual field.

That feeling of compression may also result from the viewer's sense that the plaque in some ways resembles a

medal: objects that, in the Renaissance, were often made from
bronze and might feature portraits as well as visual devices of
various kinds. Medals were generally double-sided, with the
portrait appearing on the obverse (front) and other imagery
on the reverse. Here it is as though the two sides have been
brought together into one, so that we encounter two distinct
views in a single image. The result is an uneasy amalgam: unity
and plurality, similitude and representation. Later in life,
Alberti's image would indeed appear on a medal, this time
made by a professional, his friend Matteo de' Pasti (illus. 31).
Again Alberti appears in profile gazing to the left. His face is
modelled more skilfully than in the plaque and the treatment
of his hair is so deft as to be almost painterly. The profile is
less schematic, the nose less startlingly straight, and the brow
no longer seems to arch right across the full width of the
forehead. Around the circumference his full name appears in
its Romanized form: LEO BAPTISTA ALBERTUS. On the other
side of the medal we find the winged eye, now amplified in
scale and appearing altogether more confrontational. That
confrontation is heightened by the inclusion below of Alberti's
personal motto: QUID TUM. This translates, roughly, as 'What
then?' Thus where we might expect to find a moral, or some

31 Matteo de' Pasti, medal with portrait of Leon Battista Alberti (obverse)
and winged eye (reverse), *c.* 1446–50, bronze.

cryptic saying or pithy aphorism, we are instead met with a direct challenge.

The coupling of motto and visual device seems to bespeak a fierce and untrammelled subjectivity, one that renders us the objects of an all-seeing gaze and that calls on us to account for our own existence. It resonates with a broader tendency in the writings of Alberti, an author who, despite sometimes producing normative forms of discourse, does not generally allow the reader to read normatively, seeking instead to unsettle, decentre and turn the reader's questions back on themselves. The winged eye itself is surrounded on the medal by a garland, and beyond that appears the name of its maker, Matteo de' Pasti, matching Alberti's name on the other side. There is thus a kind of third-person enframing that might be related to the contrast between the frontal and profile views discussed in relation to the plaque. In this regard, it has been suggested that the profile portrait acts as a distancing device that is comparable in its effects to literary techniques used by Alberti when he considers the self in writing.[13] The switch between first and third person is indeed characteristic of his approach, as is the assumption of personae, the donning of masks and the use of simulation and dissimulation. To see how this works, and how it might bear upon the issue of the self, we will have to turn to some more examples.

SAINT, WRITER, ORPHAN

From the outset, Alberti had displayed a marked tendency towards autobiography. Even when, as a new arrival at the papal chancellery, he was commissioned by his boss, Cardinal

Biagio Molin, the Patriarch of Grado, to write a biography of an obscure martyr saint, he could not help but turn it into an examination of the self. In Alberti's hands the life of St Potitus becomes the vehicle for a markedly dialogical exploration of virtue, fortune and glory, as well as the respective values of the active and contemplative lives – all themes that were dear to Alberti. Styling Potitus as a virtuous outsider, Alberti makes of him a type that is similar to what Mark Jarzombek has aptly dubbed the 'writer saint': a figure who recurs, in various guises, throughout Alberti's works, and who clearly relates to one aspect of his own self-image.[14]

Similar characters occur in the *Intercenales*, Alberti's collection of often strange and original Latin fables that were written over a number of years and eventually organized into eleven books. The first book begins with a very short dialogue entitled *The Writer* in which we encounter a familiar speaker, Lepidus. He converses with Libripeta (meaning 'seeker of books'), who asks why he has shut himself indoors for an entire month. When Lepidus explains that he has been 'striving to sow seeds of fame by writing' he is harshly condemned by Libripeta, who tells him that all his time has been wasted, especially since he writes in Tuscany, a land in which only the ambitious and ignorant hold sway. 'I strongly advise you against foolishly publishing your research,' warns Libripeta, 'for our vigilant and severely censorious masses are quick to condemn. And you should especially fear me. For by disparaging everyone publicly, I command more authority than if I were to praise many.'[15] The character of Libripeta is undoubtedly inspired by the Florentine Niccolò Niccoli, a Latinist and antiquarian book collector who hardly wrote himself but who extensively

critiqued the works of others, relentlessly asserting the supe-
riority of the ancients over the moderns. The notion that
both the mass of ordinary people and specialist critics stand
ready to eviscerate the writer is amply treated in *De commodis*
and the reader can have little doubt that Lepidus acts to some
extent as a proxy for Alberti himself.

The second of the *Intercenales*, entitled *The Orphan*, introduces a new and more definitively saintly character, Philoponius
(meaning 'lover of labours').[16] An orphan, exile and scholar
who has been scorned by his own family and battered by fortune's gale, he is also clearly a figure for Alberti, here appearing
in a bitter and pessimistic tale in which he laments his lot and
in which no prospect of salvation is held out. In both of these
dialogues we encounter a sense of burning injustice that, as we
will see, Alberti carried with him throughout his life. We also
meet with the insecurities that assail the majority of scholars
and writers of any kind, if not always, then at least sometimes:
hard work may bring no rewards; critics will seek every opportunity to do you down; the majority of people will be indifferent
or contemptuous; and all your labours might be wasted.

ALBERTI BY ALBERTI

These feelings of insecurity began early. However, by the time
that Alberti started writing the *Intercenales* he must already
have recognized that such doubts were not simply obstruc-
tions to his work. Rather, self-doubt was an integral part of
being a writer. Indeed, it provided material that he could
harness, refashion and put back to work in the service of his
authorial project. Through an act of literary alchemy, such

abject stuff could even become the basis of heroic myth. He attempted just such a transformation when he penned his autobiography (*Vita*) in or shortly after 1437, when he would have been around 33 years old. Needless to say, it is no straightforward account but an anonymous text written in the third person and adopting the mode of an ancient biography of a sage. Anthony Grafton has convincingly argued that Alberti took Diogenes Laertius' life of the ancient Greek philosopher Thales of Miletus as his model.[17] From the outset, the tone is laudatory. Gone is the anxiety and lamentation of *De commodis* and the *Intercenales*. In its place is a transcendent individual able to master his circumstances and himself.

'In all things proper to a freeborn man and one liberally educated,' it begins, 'he was so schooled from boyhood that he certainly never ranked last among the best.' Writer, musician, horseman, warrior, 'his mind was versatile, so much so that it seemed there was no worthy skill he had not mastered.' Far from rotting away in a library while everyone else was out dancing, the young Alberti was active and vigorous:

> He practiced ball playing, the use of the javelin with thong, running, wrestling, and above all, the climbing of steep mountains, which delighted him . . . As a youth, he excelled in military exercises: with his feet tied together, he could jump over the shoulders of a standing man; he had practically no equal in pole vaulting; the arrow his hand had drawn pierced through the strongest iron breast plate. With his left foot pressed against the very wall of the highest temple, he would throw an apple straight up far above the highest roof

of the building; inside the church, he would throw a little silver coin up with such force that whoever was with him could clearly hear it strike the interior of the loftiest dome . . . It was a strange and wonderful thing how very fierce horses, most intolerant of riders, would shudder violently when he mounted them and tremble beneath him as if in terror.[18]

In addition to all of this, the biography tells us that he practised painting and sculpture and was a self-taught musician who grew so proficient that he was able to instruct others. He had no interest in money, shared his knowledge freely with anyone who desired it, and was courteous with everyone despite receiving more than his measure of envy and hatred. Learned men respected him and princes admired him. Others collected his spontaneous remarks, pithy repositories of wisdom and wit that are listed in the *Vita* at some length (and some of which are lifted straight from ancient sources).

This is the heroic portrait on which Burckhardt based his image of Alberti as the arch-Renaissance individual and *uomo universale* (universal man). Yet Alberti does not banish all traces of struggle and doubt. On the contrary, these things are martialled to demonstrate his extraordinary ability to overcome adversity. He relates how, during his study of law, he became ill on account of overwork and the harsh treatment that he received from some of his relatives. Once recovered, he took up the law again, only to be struck down by an even greater affliction: 'As he was reading, the keenness of his eyesight suddenly failed, and he was overcome with dizziness and pain while a roaring and loud ringing filled his ears.'

Ignoring medical advice to desist from work, he exacerbated the condition until 'he fell into an illness worthy of memory. For at this time he could not recall the names of the most familiar things, as if these would be of no further use to him, but he retained a miraculously firm grasp of anything he saw.'[19] Forced, temporarily, to quit the study of law, he instead took up mathematics and physics – subjects that involved less memorization – as a form of intellectual nourishment while he recovered. The anxiety of scholarly work is thus fully present, as is the mental fragility that the scholar must endure. However, Alberti is able to overcome these things, achieving mastery of the world and mastery of himself.

Self-mastery in fact emerges as one of the predominant themes of the *Vita*. Alberti says that he was able to withstand great pain without complaint. He treated his own wounds, and he even cured a terrible fever through singing. He also managed to build resistance to that most mysterious of Italian afflictions: a *colpo d'aria*, or a blast of air, something that is often credited with the power to bring on maladies of all kinds:

He had by nature a head that could not stand the slightest cold and draft. By gradually developing the habit in summer, he got so that he could ride about bareheaded in winter, no matter how fierce the wind. Likewise, by some fault of his constitution he abhorred both garlic and honey, so that the mere sight of these things, when chance put them before him, could make him nauseous. But he overcame these weaknesses by dint of looking at and handling the undesired things, until finally he could take them perfectly well – thus illustrating the truth that men can make of themselves whatever they want to, if they have the will.[20]

That act of willing – what we might today, following Nietzsche, call 'will to power' – could be extended to all aspects of life. Thus Alberti tells us that he deliberately created a finely crafted public appearance, paying attention to every aspect of his behaviour:

> He was always examining his own conduct, checking it again and again to make sure there was nothing there to make anyone even suspect any ill of him . . . he wanted everything in his life, every gesture and every word, to be, as well as to seem to be, the expression of one who merits the good will of good men, and he would say that, as in everything, so especially in these three things one should take the utmost care, adding art to art to make the result seem free of artifice – how one walks in the street, how one rides, and how one speaks; in these things one should make every effort to be pleasing to all.[21]

This studied effortlessness might seem to anticipate the courtly form of artificially wrought natural ease that in the following century Baldassare Castiglione would describe with the wonderful word *sprezzatura*. It also speaks to the broader tendency that Stephen Greenblatt has memorably termed 'self-fashioning', the meticulous process of creating a public persona that has come to play such a key role in our understanding of the Renaissance psyche.[22] Upon encountering such a well-fashioned self, one might admire the ease and confidence that it radiated, even as one also marvelled at the hidden effort that must have been employed in order to create it. That effort, more than anything, is what Alberti vaunts in the *Vita*. We are to behold his industriousness and his diligence, and wonder at his extraordinary feats of self-overcoming.

What was all of this in aid of? To impress in public, and to be well thought of, certainly. But Alberti's public persona was also a carapace to help him withstand what he considered to be the inevitable attacks of the malevolent and the envious. He crafted his conduct, including all of the subtle non-linguistic cues embedded in everyday acts such as walking – the 'body language' to which he ascribed such significance in *De pictura* – so as to avoid all suspicion. For as he said: 'slanderers inject the worst of evils into human life. These, as he would say, besmirch the reputation of good men not only because of resentment and enmity, but also for mere amusement and malicious pleasure, yet nothing can eradicate the scars left by the wounds they make.'[23] Alberti's self-mastery was thus by turns triumphant and defensive, the product of both a transcendent will and a fragile psyche. There is much in the *Vita* regarding the attacks of wicked men, and Alberti tells how he had to learn to rein in his emotions, since

he himself was by nature quite irascible and had a quick temper; but he deliberately repressed his rising indignation immediately, and he purposely avoided the verbose and obstinate persons with whom he could not help growing hot with anger. At other times he deliberately exposed himself to shameless impudence just to teach himself patience.[24]

Some of the maxims that Alberti employs in this regard, such as 'Men can make of themselves whatever they want to, if they have the will,' might to modern readers smack of the kind of pseudo-inspirational language beloved of self-help manuals and management training courses. However, this is simply because those modern discourses themselves echo, albeit in a debased and superficial way, some aspects of the Stoic philosophical tradition to which Alberti was deeply attached. This tradition emphasized the importance of the moral resources that individuals carried within themselves and the power that those resources provided to overcome external circumstances, but it also fully acknowledged the depth of human frailty and considered the actions that one might take to calm an unquiet mind. In this spirit, Alberti sometimes presents his undertakings as something like pharmacological treatments for a damaged soul. It is towards the start of the *Vita* that he confesses to a divided attitude towards scholarship and writing, saying that he was sometimes consumed with the love of letters, while at other times the words piled up under his eyes like scorpions. In the latter case, 'he would shift his attention to music and painting and physical exercise.'[25] In the flow of these activities, he was perhaps able to find tranquillity, as suggested by his remark in *De pictura* that, when he painted, many hours would pass without him noticing. Yet writing too could be consolatory, and he tells us that he wrote the *Philodoxeos* during the first of his nervous breakdowns at university, when illness had forced

him temporarily to quit the law and when he was distraught
at the poor treatment he received from his relatives.

Burckhardt did not include this aspect of Alberti in his
literary portrait. The character he described was the transcendent artist-intellectual and athlete who mastered both
himself and the world. The damaged and fragile individual
who anxiously protected himself from slanderous attacks, and
who sought to alleviate the symptoms of his mental anguish,
was suppressed. Instead the Swiss historian held up Alberti's
universality as the ultimate achievement of the individual will.
Alberti's contemporaries had also remarked on his breadth
of expertise. His schoolfriend and fellow humanist Lapo da
Castiglionchio the Younger marvelled at Alberti's apparent
ability effortlessly and instantly to master any field to which
he turned his attention.[26] After his death, the writer Cristoforo
Landino, a fellow author and friend of Alberti, commented
that 'I remember the style of Battista Alberto, who like a new
chameleon always assumes the colours of what he writes
about.'[27] This description of Alberti as a chameleon acknowledges the diversity of his interests but it is less straightforwardly
heroic than the idea of the universal man. With its overtones
of camouflage and artifice, it offers a more indeterminate and
ambiguous approach to Alberti's multiform nature, which now
becomes something altogether more difficult to pin down.

Perhaps Landino was prompted to reach for the simile by
Alberti's own words in *De pictura*, a text that he probably knew.
In the Tuscan version Alberti had noted that what he called
the 'median rays' of the visual pyramid (those rays that strike
the interiors of surfaces and carry colours to the eye) 'act in
the same way as the chameleon is said to – an animal that

assumes the colour of everything that is near to it'.[28] The comparison is a straightforward one, but it is worth noting that Alberti elaborated upon it in the Latin version, observing: 'these rays do what they say the chameleon and other like beasts are wont to do when struck with fear, who assume the colours of nearby objects so as not to be discovered by hunters.'[29] This substantially broadens the range of signification and perhaps points the way towards a clearer understanding of Alberti's many-sidedness. His chameleonic nature was marvellous and extraordinary, without doubt, but it was not unconnected to the fear that dwelt within the mind of one who felt himself to be 'hunted' by men of ill will.

FLIES, EYES AND EAGLES

In a short piece of writing that he dedicated to the same Landino, Alberti had employed a different animal in order to comment obliquely on his own versatility. *Musca* is a comic work praising what is usually ranked among the lowliest of insects: the fly.[30] It takes its inspiration from the paradoxical encomium on the same subject by the Greek-Syrian writer Lucian of Samosata, which had only recently been translated into Latin by another humanist, Guarino da Verona, with a dedication to Alberti. When the latter produced his own version, some time before 1443, it was thus part of a complex humanist discourse involving the rediscovery, translation, imitation and transformation of ancient texts. That discourse was not a dry one but was, on the contrary, lively and personal. Alberti told Landino that he received Guarino's translation while he was in the grips of a harsh fever, and he claimed that the humour it contained brought him great relief. It also inspired him to dictate, then and there, his own *Musca* to some of his friends; a process that caused him so much laughter that the sweat disappeared from his brow and he was entirely cured. So delighted were all of those present that they decided to send it on so that Landino could laugh too. The literary, then, could be intensely personal, and the personal could be literary. Thus Alberti would continue to reach for literary commonplaces even when describing his most personal experiences (the *Vita* contains many such examples) and, contrarily, would reach for personal experiences when undertaking what might at first seem only to be literary exercises. *The Fly* is no exception.

Among the many outstanding virtues that Alberti attributes to the fly, he dwells particularly on its unquenchable thirst for knowledge. Given to philosophizing and naturally predisposed towards 'researching and understanding things', the fly seeks to enter into all the mysteries of nature, from the deepest recesses of the earth to the highest reaches of the heavens, so that 'even the most hidden secrets do not escape its investigations'.[31] This sounds admirable indeed but every time it is touched upon it is immediately undercut. What is known to the fly includes the smallest defects on the buttocks of Helen of Troy and the most secret parts of Ganymede. These things are humorous in their triviality while also pointing towards the more serious idea that the lofty desire for knowledge is in truth not so different from the base desire for bodily pleasures. If this sounds like satire, then it is satire directed squarely at the author. The creature that would know everything, and that enquires into every field, cannot help but remind us of

Alberti. The connection appears even stronger when we consider how he frames this quest for knowledge in terms of the fly's physical attributes. For he notes that it is 'gifted by nature with enormous eyes', which take up a much greater proportion of its head than is the case with human beings. With eyes of this size, he wonders, what could ever escape the fly's great curiosity? One does not have to read too far between the lines to understand that the fly is essentially a winged eye. As such, it is the satirical counterpart to Alberti's own visual device, and we might speculate that the physical relief that Alberti drew from composing his encomium must have been connected to a more fundamental emotional relief deriving from the humorous treatment of his own literary practices (practices that, as he repeatedly tells us, were in reality fraught with anxiety). The author who extolled the self in the *Vita* was thus also quite capable of self-mockery; of seeing the 'other side' of his many-sidedness, and indeed of understanding that many-sidedness as itself being a many-sided idea.

If Alberti was borne aloft on flies' wings, however, he was also sustained by mightier appendages. Among the *Intercenales*, one that is entitled *Anuli* (*Rings*) provides a different account of the winged eye. This dialogue was never incorporated into any of the eleven books. It was probably written quite early on, perhaps in the first years of the 1430s, around the time that Alberti adopted his new name. In it, we again meet the troubled orphan-scholar Philoponius, who is now in a state of utter dejection, fearing that all of his literary efforts have been in vain. Brought before Minerva by his companions Hope, Counsel and Genius, he is assured by the goddess that he has in reality succeeded well. As proof of this, a series of rings that he has made, inscribed with allegorical images, are presented and described, and the very first of these features a crown that has in its centre an eye attached to an eagle's wing. Explaining the image, Counsel says: 'The crown is an emblem of gladness and glory. There is nothing more powerful, swift, or worthy than the eye. In short, it is the foremost of the body's members, a sort of king or god. Didn't the ancients regard God as similar to the eye, since he surveys all things and reckons them singly?'[32] From this, Counsel continues, it is obvious that we should remain vigilant and seek the glory of virtue, relying on our own industry to achieve things that are noble and divine. In this first ring, then, Alberti signals that the mysteries that are explained here are closely connected to his own sense of self, since they begin with his personal emblem and announce an aspiration towards a higher level of knowledge.

Among the other rings, one in particular stands out, since Counsel describes it as 'the most beautiful of all'. On it, 'there is an unbroken circle. Within it is inscribed "YOURSELF. TO YOU. AND. TO GOD." Outside the circle, there is a hook and a blazing flame.' Explaining this, Counsel says, 'there is nothing more capacious, more whole, or more durable than the circle. At every point it is perfectly suited to repelling blows, and its motion is the freest of all figures. We must remain within the safe and free circle of reason, that is, within humanity. For virtue is bound and tied to humanity, and God to virtue, which proceeds from God.'[33] Outside of the circle are the hooks of pleasure, the fires of wrath and the flames of desire, all of which must be banished from our lives. Here we encounter another figure for the self, as is signalled by the inscription, which begins with the Latin words 'TE. TIBI', signalling that *you* are at the centre. The self in question seems to be an essential one, considered as a circle, which, so long as it remains pure and perfectly formed, can repel any blows it might receive – presumably the blows of fortune and the insults and slanders that Alberti describes in the *Vita*. Disturbing passions such as rage must be expelled, just as we know that Alberti sought to do, and excessive desire – that central theme of his early writings – should also be excluded. What remains is the rational self, untroubled by perturbations of the soul. However, this should not be thought of simply as an isolated point, since the circle is also described as signifying *humanitas* and is in that sense indistinguishable from 'humanness', or humanity as a whole. Alberti knew that these things were inseparable, and his considerations of selfhood are always inextricably linked to broader concerns regarding society. With this in mind, we will now shift our attention from the self to the most fundamental social unit with which Alberti was involved: the family.

FIVE

The Family

o be a prominent citizen of the Florentine republic was a tricky business. It required ostentation, but not too much. Wealth and power demanded to be shown, yet one man's magnificence was another man's vainglory. For those who became so big that they forgot restraint, trouble might beckon. The Alberti knew this well. It was not only Benedetto's hardball politicking that had brought them to disaster, but the family's immense spending on public festivities. How many richly caparisoned horses, decorated with the Alberti coat of arms, could one contribute to a procession before it began to look more like a celebration of the family than the city?[1] The Alberti learnt the answer to this question the hard way.

When it came to big spending, buildings loomed large. A family needed a palace to house it and to anchor it in a place: things that both demonstrated and helped to foster its longevity. The Alberti had colonized most of a long stretch of via de' Benci, a prominent street running from the river to the Basilica of Santa Croce (illus. 32 and 33), and in the fourteenth century Benedetto had built a fine but sober home there for his branch of the family (illus. 34).[2] A well-designed palace could announce the grandeur of its occupants while at the

32 Alberti tower and loggia, which constituted the main focus in the long line of Alberti buildings along via de' Benci, in the parish of San Iacopo tra le Fosse, Gonfalone of Lion Nero, Florence.

same time, by conforming to the appearance of other, similar buildings, express a conservative sense of belonging. The trick was to make one's mark while fitting in. By the time Alberti moved to Florence in the 1430s, another factor had to be weighed. Cosimo de' Medici had returned from a brief exile in 1434 and his family had assumed an unprecedented level of dominance in the city. In 1444 he commissioned the sculptor and architect Michelozzo Michelozzi to build a grand palace on via Larga (now via Cavour; illus. 35). Allegedly he rejected a more ambitious design by Brunelleschi for fear that it might arouse envy; an act that Vasari claims caused the architect to destroy his own model in a fit of rage. In any case, what was eventually constructed was far from inconspicuous, being of great size and including rusticated facades, 'bifore' windows (divided into two separate openings by a column) and a giant, antique-feeling cornice. Other aspiring builders took note.

One such observer was the merchant banker Giovanni di Paolo Rucellai. In 1448 he began a building campaign of his

33 Column capital from the Alberti loggia, via de' Benci. The capitals, which display crossed chains, the heraldic emblem of the Alberti family, are probably replacements, likely following an earlier model.

own, starting with the acquisition of properties around his house, seven of which he would eventually amalgamate into a magnificent palace (illus. 36). Tradition has it that Alberti was the architect of the facade, yet no document links him to the building until the sixteenth century. While many architectural historians have accepted Alberti's authorship, an alternative tradition, descending from Julius von Schlosser, rejects it. Some, pointing to similarities with the Palazzo Piccolomini in Pienza, suggest that its designer, Bernardo Rossellino, must have been responsible for both projects, especially since another late fifteenth- or early sixteenth-century source – the *Libro di Antonio Billi*, the very first to make an attribution – names only Rossellino as the architect (illus. 37). Against this, others have emphasized the very significant differences of approach that each building reveals.[3] The patterning of the stonework alone is more complex at the Rucellai palace by several orders of magnitude – something that cannot be accounted for

34 Palace of Benedetto di Nerozzo Alberti, on the corner of via de' Benci and Borgo Santa Croce, Florence.

35 Michelozzo Michelozzi, Palazzo Medici Riccardi, begun 1444,
subsequently extended to the north, via Cavour, Florence.

36 Alberti (attributed), Palazzo Rucellai on via della Vigna Nuova,
Florence, designed after 1448.

simply by the differences in materials or the skills of local craftsmen, and that, according to some observers, is telling of a different architectural intelligence altogether. Of course, arguments based upon connoisseurial appraisals are necessarily weak, since there are insufficient buildings by Alberti on which to found firm judgements, and since his method was so manifestly contextual that we should anyway expect his works to differ markedly from one to the next depending upon building type and location (as indeed they do). Needless to say, the matter cannot be settled here, if it can be settled at all, but the palace can certainly fruitfully be understood within the broader context of Alberti's intellectual outlook. For, in a sense, it does for the Rucellai family what Alberti did for himself in the *Vita*, employing conventions drawn from antiquity in order to construct something markedly contemporary.

The Palazzo Rucellai was both comfortingly familiar and startlingly novel. Its facade is made of the traditional, brown *pietra forte* sandstone that one finds throughout Florence.

37 Bernardo Rossellino, Palazzo Piccolomini, Pienza, begun 1459 and completed by 1462.

Like the Palazzo Medici, it is divided into three storeys that gradually diminish in height as they ascend. All of them are rusticated, which is to say that the masonry has been drafted to give the impression of many individual blocks (although, while each one corresponds in height to the real blocks used in construction, one block is often divided lengthwise so that it appears as if it were two). Also like the Palazzo Medici, the palace displays bifore windows on its upper two storeys and is capped off with a large cornice, an expensive feature that required heavy stonework to be knitted into the fabric of the building. Some things, however, are entirely new. The whole facade is articulated by an ornamental scheme derived from Roman architecture, made up of pilasters – the vertical elements that look like flat, rectilinear columns – and entablatures, the long stonework bands that the pilasters appear to support. These belong to what are usually referred to today as the architectural 'orders', and although they were far from unknown at the time, Florentine Renaissance architects had not hitherto used them as exterior decoration for domestic buildings. On the Palazzo Rucellai, they combine with the drafted masonry to bring relief, generating a constant play of light and shade. They also create a taut, proportional nexus that runs across the entire facade, since it is now divided into bays of exactly equal size, with the exception of the entrance bays, which are slightly wider. It has been suggested that initially the facade consisted of just five bays, which would have located the entrance in the centre. Later, according to this argument, after another property had been obtained, a further two bays were added, with the edge left 'ragged' in anticipation of still further expansion.[4]

The facade establishes a lively formal tension between the grid of the orders and what seems at first glance to be the more haphazard pattern of the drafted masonry within each bay. In fact, closer inspection reveals that the drafted blocks have been arranged according to a highly sophisticated system that would have required fashioning each one on the ground before setting it on the facade – a process that must have been rather like a fiendishly complex puzzle.[5] The finished effect is striking, appearing simultaneously ancient and modern. Even now the building stands out against the urban fabric around it, and it must have done so a great deal more when it was first made. The prominent grid described by the pilasters and entablatures seems to proclaim that, although it is part of the city, the facade nonetheless operates according to an autonomous

38 Forum of Augustus, Rome, 25–2 BCE. The tall fire wall is visible at the back.

order that belongs to the discipline of architecture and that draws its inspiration from the distant past.

Just as one could have an ancient-style biography to frame one's life, so one could erect an ancient-style facade to present one's family to the world, appropriating an enduring tradition while simultaneously assuming an untimeliness that was polemically contemporary. Cosimo de' Medici seems to have wanted something of this kind, if we are to believe an early sixteenth-century source that claims he adopted heavily rusticated outer walls (the word itself denotes 'roughness') in order to imitate the 'Forum of Trajan' in Rome (in fact probably the rough tufa wall built to protect the Forum of Augustus from fires in the adjacent popular district of the Suburra (illus. 38)).[6] Following a period in the political wilderness, Giovanni Rucellai eventually established good relations with the Medici (literally, since the two families intermarried) but he was not himself in the business of rulership or governing and had less motivation to turn to such imperial models. Nonetheless he made note of Cicero's report of the building project of an ancient Roman senator on the Palatine Hill, and perhaps saw it as a fitting precedent for his own activities.[7] Giovanni was intensely concerned with his business, with the prosperity of his family and with the propagation of his name. As the author of a records book, the *Zibaldone quaresimale*, that combined financial accounts with personal reflections and reports of memorable events (he himself described it as a 'salad of mixed leaves'), Giovanni emerges as a strong personality: shrewd, cultured and intensely family-oriented; a charismatic *paterfamilias* with a particular interest in the question of family structure and the relationship between fathers and sons.[8] These were interests that Alberti shared.

Upon his banishment in 1401, Lorenzo Alberti went to Genoa, where he owned a bank. The forged Genoese document that purports to identify Alberti's mother describes Lorenzo as rolling into town somewhat like a rock star, relating that he 'had a perfect face and body, and was greatly loved by everybody on account of his wealth and liberality'. As a result, it says, he was able to take as a lover 'the noble and beautiful' widow Bianchina, with whom he fathered Carlo and Battista.[9] Of course, this might well be pure fantasy on the part of the forger, but Lorenzo must indeed have been a commanding figure. When he married the Florentine Margherita Benini in 1408, the Genoese authorities facilitated the celebrations by suspending the sumptuary codes for three days, so that women could wear real pearls and both men and women could dress in silks of all kinds and colours. Moreover, during the same three days they blocked all of the streets leading to the Piazza Banchi, where the festivities took place, and mandated that all of the businesses operating there stay closed. This near-unprecedented three-day shutdown of the centre of the entire Ligurian financial system amply testifies to Lorenzo's exalted status.[10] If Lorenzo was a larger-than-life character, the young Alberti certainly seems to have been devoted to him. A letter from Battista's Paduan teacher, Gasparino Barzizza, probably written in 1417, urges Lorenzo to leave Venice, where the plague was raging, and come to Padua, since the thirteen-year-old

Battista was sick with worry.[11] The death of his father under-
standably presented a terrible prospect to the adolescent
schoolboy. And although he could not have known it, it was
in truth not far off, since an illness would end Lorenzo's life
on 28 May 1421, when Battista was just seventeen years old.

This was the great catastrophe of Alberti's life, registered
in various ways in his literary activities. In the later commentary to the *Philodoxeos*, he says that he wrote the play as a form
of therapy following Lorenzo's death.[12] The *De commodis* too
begins by evoking Lorenzo's name. In fact, the very first sentence of the opening address to Carlo begins: 'Our parent
Lorenzo was, in his day, easily the wisest of all the Alberti
clan, among other things, in the way he raised his children,
and as you remember, Carlo, he reminded us never to be idle
in public or private, and never to seem so.'[13] In that work, the
ironic self-portrait of the scholar appears almost diametrically
opposed to the image of the rich and influential business-
man that emerges from Lorenzo's wedding celebrations, as
though the author was seeking, through hyperbole, to come
to terms with the existence of an unbearable and unbridgeable
distance.

Perhaps it was wonderful to be the son of a man like
Lorenzo; perhaps it was also hard, especially when the son was
a bastard. Lorenzo's will directed that Carlo and Battista
should each be paid a sum of 4,000 gold ducats. It was a large
amount of money, but that was it. Lorenzo expressly forbade
(*proybens expresse*) that his illegitimate sons should, under any
circumstances, ever inherit any familial assets: that is to say,
no property and no share of the businesses. Lorenzo's third of
the paternal inheritance was to be divided between his nephew

Benedetto di Bernardo and his brother Ricciardo. The former received one-third and the latter two-thirds. Lorenzo's stakes in the family companies in London and Bruges were to be wound up and, once his obligations were settled, the remaining profits would be paid to Ricciardo, his executor and universal heir. Everything, in other words, went back into the legitimate line of the family descending from Benedetto di Nerozzo. Battista and Carlo now became wards of their uncle Ricciardo, but he died the following year (1422). Their financial affairs passed into the hands of their two cousins, Benedetto di Bernardo, then aged 34, and Antonio di Ricciardo, just eighteen years old, residents of Padua and Bologna respectively.[14] Rapidly, then, the innermost circle of kinship vanished and Lorenzo's sons had to fall back upon weaker bonds of familiarity. By the mid-1430s those bonds had frayed beyond repair. Antonio and Benedetto had to support their cousin Battista during his university studies, but they prevaricated over the legacy. The lump sums – those 4,000 gold ducats each for Battista and Carlo – were never paid out.

The intense bitterness of the resulting dispute is attested to in several of Alberti's works, from *The Orphan*, examined briefly above, through the commentary to the *Philodoxeos*, to the *Momus* of his later years. If it is masked, in some cases, by the thinnest layer of dissimulation – or at least distanced by the conventions of fiction – it is raw and direct in other texts, including the *Vita*. There, he speaks of the 'troublesome secret intrigues, bitter offences, and intolerable humiliations inflicted especially by his own relatives'.[15] His enemies, he lamented, subjected him to terrible calumnies, so bitterly did they resent the fact that one whose fortune they had taken a great deal of trouble to keep well below their own surpassed them in virtue and reputation. There were even some among his relatives (to say nothing of others) who, after receiving favours and generous help from him, were ungrateful and cruel enough to conspire in a dreadful internecine crime, inciting servants to assault him boldly with a barbarous knife.[16]

This suggests an attempt on his life, an idea that appears to be supported by a contemporary letter, although the wording is cryptic.[17] The rapid deterioration of these family relations can be traced to the mid-1430s, but tensions may have begun much earlier, since Alberti ascribes his first breakdown at university not only to overwork but to 'the inhumanity and lack of conscience of his relatives'.[18]

In *The Orphan* such harsh treatment forms the prevailing theme. Wicked relatives, he says, tried to prevent Philoponius from pursuing his vocation as a scholar in every way that they could. When others rebuked them for their bad behaviour, they offered neither denials nor justifications but simply carried on in their own arrogant ways, and 'they foolishly asserted that anyone merited disdain who wished his literary achievements to win him more esteem than wealthy men possessed.'[19] The remark is a telling one. Unlike his brother Carlo, Battista had chosen not to enter the family business but had decided instead to try to make it as a writer, and it may be that he was forced to endure barbs from his wealthy, legitimate cousins who saw his activities as worthless and his studies as a burdensome expense. In 1433 Antonio submitted a declaration to Florentine tax officials, in which he named Battista and Carlo as debtors to the Bruges company, from which he had been compelled to make advances in his own name to support them, 'for books, and to support their studies, and to clothe them, and for other things'.[20] He made no mention of the 8,000 gold ducats they were still owed from Lorenzo's legacy.

By the time that Alberti wrote the *Vita*, matters had worsened. Any pride that the cousins might have felt as financiers was not matched by talent, and by 1437 they had driven the Alberti businesses into the ground. Both the company of the Ponente, which comprised the operations in London, Bruges and Cologne, and the company of the 'corte' di Roma, which served the papal court and which also maintained a branch in Basel, were ultimately undone. Trouble erupted spectacularly in April 1436, when Francesco d'Altobianco Alberti, the cousins' partner in the Rome company, successfully petitioned the authorities in Pisa and Livorno to seize a huge consignment of wool, valued at around 7,750 florins. The wool had been obtained by the London bank from William Willey, a merchant of Camden, and was destined for sale in Italy. Francesco d'Altobianco claimed that the company of the 'corte' was owed 17,000 florins by the Ponente, where Benedetto di Bernardo and Antonio di Ricciardo were the men in charge. While matters were swiftly resolved between these parties, other creditors rapidly piled in with further lawsuits, all attempting to impound the wool themselves. William Willey was never able to recover his losses.

Over the following year, it became clear that the Ponente business was in very poor shape. Legal disputes of various kinds began to multiply, pitting Francesco d'Altobianco against

Benedetto and Antonio, turning managers against their Alberti bosses and causing angry creditors to launch claims against managers and bosses alike. Time and again, litigants decried the incompetence and dishonesty of the two cousins. By March 1437, the situation was dire. Benedetto di Bernardo had fled from Florence, the manager of the London bank had been thrown in jail, and numerous creditors had launched legal actions. Meanwhile, in the Florentine merchants' tribunal, the Mercanzia, Francesco d'Altobianco and Antonio di Ricciardo conducted an exceptionally bitter dispute in which they assassinated each other's character and contested everything from debts worth thousands of florins to the exact value of a half-blind mule.[21]

Companies that had survived and even thrived under the conditions of exile thus endured only a short time following the Alberti's readmission to Florence. By 1442 Antonio would be writing in his tax return: 'my assets have been robbed and taken from me, and I have nothing left, nothing except seven children and a debt that, between what I owe the *comune* and others, amounts to maybe 30,000 florins.' After 1437 the family never recovered its former position, either financially or politically.[22]

ON THE FAMILY

Family relations, then, were difficult. However, as Luca Boschetto has recently demonstrated, we should not imagine that Alberti was estranged.[23] On the contrary, he maintained close and often warm relations with several members of the Alberti family. Moreover, he dedicated significant attention to the idea of the family itself. Already, before arriving in Florence, he had started work on a treatise entitled *De familia*, or *On the Family*. In the *Vita*, he says that he wrote the first three books of *De familia* in Rome in a period of only ninety days, though it seems certain that the preface to the third book cannot have been drafted before the spring of 1435 when he was already in Florence and it might be that all of Book III dates from that year. It might thus be grouped together with the *De pictura*, the letter to Brunelleschi, the bronze plaque and other works as part of an intense moment of creative energy unleashed by his transferral to the city.[24] The treatise was also his first really large work in the Tuscan language. It is in the form of a dialogue, and the participants are nearly all members of the Alberti family. Penned in an approachable, even conversational style (though at times highly Latinate), it was popular, though in a strange way. From the 1450s the third book quickly began to appear separately under the name of Agnolo Pandolfini (a speaker in the *Profugiorum*) and circulated quite widely as such. Giovanni Rucellai apparently owned a copy, and he transcribed some lengthy sections into his *Zibaldone*. In 1437 Alberti would add a further, fourth book to complete the work. In the *Vita*, he says that he composed the first three books specifically for his relatives, and that he rendered it 'in the paternal Tuscan to help those who were ignorant of Latin'.[25] Apparently the gesture was not appreciated, since he continues:

> When he gave the first three books of *De familia* to his kinsmen to read, he took it ill that among all the Alberti, amply endowed with leisure, scarcely one deigned even

to peruse the titles, at the very time that these books were in demand among foreign nations. He could not help being angry when he discovered that some among his relatives openly scoffed at the whole work and at the author as inept. Because of this affront he was determined, had not certain princes interfered, to burn the three books he had then completed. Eventually, however, duty overcame indignation, and, after three years, he offered the ingrates a fourth volume. 'If you are virtuous,' he wrote, 'you will appreciate and love me, but if lacking in virtue, your bad character will make you hated.'[26]

If Alberti had hoped for familial approval, then, he was disappointed. In fact, his motives for writing in the first place seem to have been mixed. Undoubtedly he takes the opportunity in the treatise to rebuke, with various degrees of subtlety, those family members he felt had abused him, although they do not appear as characters. On the other hand, he goes to great pains to defend the family as a whole (what Florentines called the *consortería*) and to heap praise upon his own ancestors. And as with some of his other early works, it all starts with Lorenzo.

'While our father Lorenzo Alberti was ill in Padua with that last infirmity which took him away from us,' the first book begins, 'he wished for many days to see his brother Ricciardo Alberti.' Upon being told that Ricciardo would soon arrive, Lorenzo took heart, sat up in bed more than usual and began to speak to the members of the family assembled there: Adovardo and Lionardo Alberti, and his sons Battista and Carlo. He told them that he wished to arrange some family matters with Ricciardo and, above all, to urge him to take good care of his two sons (as he knew that Ricciardo would): 'to guide them in becoming good men and do for them what, if the need arose, you would want done for your own children in order to make them virtuous'.[27] Conversing with Adovardo, Lorenzo then enters into a lengthy discourse regarding the role of the head of the family, in which he also recalls the advice of his own father Benedetto. From the outset, there is an appeal to familial bonds – fraternal, parental, filial and avuncular – and an emphasis on the unbroken lineage that connects the generations from Benedetto to Battista. Pointedly the Alberti are reminded of their duty to Battista and Carlo, which is also a duty to Lorenzo, since it constitutes his dying wish.

This deathbed scene, in which Alberti reanimated his deceased father in writing (a power, raising the dead, that he would ascribe to painting in the *De pictura*), must have been intensely meaningful for him. It also establishes the context for the entire treatise, which takes place in the shadow of this event. Following Lorenzo's speech, doctors arrive urging him to rest. The other characters retire to another room and it is at this point that the dialogue proper begins. Each of the four books contains discussions of key themes relating to the family, and to life more broadly. Loosely speaking, the first book considers the duties that different generations of the family owe to each other, and expands upon the importance of a liberal education. The main speakers are Adovardo, an older man and the father of four children, and the unmarried Lionardo, who would have been about 29 at the time and who is presented as a humanist intellectual. The second book turns to the theme of love and marriage, with much of the conversation taking place between Lionardo and the seventeen-year-old Battista himself, though he deferentially allows his older relative much more space to expound his views. The third book, which, unlike the others, comes with a preface of its own, turns to the subject of household economy. The conversation takes place the following day, and while Lionardo stays on, his chief interlocutor is now Giannozzo Alberti, a wise and elderly merchant and head of a large household. Later on, they are joined again by Adovardo. In the fourth book, on the topic of friendship, there is a brief, comic appearance by the family retainer Buto. Piero Alberti, a kind of professional courtier, joins the discussion and Lionardo and Adovardo continue as speakers.

It is impossible, in a short summary, to do justice to a work of such richness and depth. *De família* is truly dialogical in character. Lionardo is the most consistently present and, as a young humanist, might be expected to act as Alberti's spokesman. In fact, things are more complex, with all of the speakers advancing credible positions, including when they disagree. Within the structure outlined above, they touch upon many topics. In the first two books, these include the merits of different professions, the relative values of money-making and scholarship, the vices to which the young might fall prey, the raising of children, the importance of breastfeeding, the nature of love, marriage and sexual desire, the practice of adoption, and more. The third book stands out for the intensity of the debate and also for the character of Giannozzo, brilliantly drawn by Alberti as a compelling portrait of a Renaissance merchant and patriarch. Importantly, Giannozzo is not a humanist or a scholar of any kind – a point that he emphazises repeatedly by contrasting his own approach with that of Lionardo and Adovardo, whom he often calls 'you men of letters'. In these conversations, practical and humanist discourses meet and are tested against each other, with Giannozzo's trump card, experience, often winning the day. That is not to say that his speech is genuinely free of humanist reasoning. It is, after all, written by Alberti. As such, it contains rhetorical flourishes (including its own conspicuous disavowal of eloquence) and is often guided by Ciceronian models, Epicurean philosophy and other intellectual influences. However, it also utilizes direct observation of the social world of the patriarch, and it serves to stage the encounter between two distinct forms of knowledge. That encounter is crucial for grasping Alberti's intellectual outlook: his understanding of humanism's restrictions, the limitations of eloquence, and the value of other epistemological approaches. At times, it gives voice to the anti-humanism that constituted a significant part of Alberti's humanism: an anti-humanism that he often framed in thoroughly humanist terms.

Here, such framing is made explicit at the outset. In the preface, addressed to his kinsman Francesco d'Altobianco, Alberti says that he sought 'to imitate the melodious and mellow style of the Greek writer Xenophon', a student of Socrates who was the author of a dialogue known, in its Latinized form, as the *Oeconomicus* (The Economist).[28] While we might, these days, more readily associate economics with the management of a state, the word derives from the Greek *oíkos*, signifying the house, and both Xenophon and Alberti are concerned with it in that sense. The subject, then, is household management, or what Giannozzo calls *masserízia*. If this sounds like something of little consequence, think again. It is a matter of the highest importance: 'santa cosa la masserizia!' (*masserizia* is a sacred thing!) exclaims Giannozzo.[29] Conversing with Lionardo, he addresses topics such as how to choose a city in which to live (a pressing question for exiles), whether to rent or to buy (always buy), whether the extended family should live together or apart (together as much as possible), how to obtain food (things produced on your own properties will be superior to what can be bought at the market), the relative merits of the country and the city (the country is best), and how to behave towards one's wife (strictly).

This last topic was also treated by Xenophon, but Alberti addresses it with particular energy. Giannozzo explains how he introduced his wife into his household and taught her to become an effective and obedient manager in an account that is animated by a powerful strain of misogyny and that seems to go well beyond the standard chauvinism of the age. It is not an isolated case in Alberti's writings but rather one of a series of instances in which he characterizes women as vain, vacuous, and in need of constant correction. While his real attitude towards women continues to be debated by scholars, there is no doubt that these passages make for very uncomfortable reading. The wife must be closely observed, clearly instructed and reproved when necessary. This should serve to remind us that the society of fifteenth-century Italy was a deeply unequal one, structured around relationships of servitude and mastery. The Florentine republic did not grant women political rights. Workers were subject to draconian laws, and Florentine men of the Alberti's class – including the cousins Antonio and Benedetto – were often slave-owners. Domination and exploitation were standard fare.

The patrilineal and patriarchal nature of the Alberti family is writ large throughout *De familia*. The women of the *consorteria* receive little acknowledgement, though in reality they played a crucial role in preserving the clan's ties to Florence in the decades of exile. Giannozzo's relations with his wife point towards a conception of the self that, while it is thoroughly embedded in the family, is also remarkably isolated and self-contained. Thus he explains that he keeps all of his important papers under lock and key, and makes sure that none of them are known to his wife. This coheres with a broader tendency towards self-reliance and control. A wealthy family like the Alberti would normally own a range of country properties – often productive ones managed by tenant-farmers – each of which could be referred to by the generic term *villa*. In *De familia*, Giannozzo dreams of an autarchic existence at the villa, freed from the communal obligations of the city. This is a logical extreme, employed for the sake of argument, since Giannozzo is a man of affairs, the director of a great business and someone who must deal with the civic authorities. At his entrance to the dialogue, he explains that only that morning he had gone to the government palace (perhaps the Palazzo della Ragione in Padua) on behalf of a friend. His advice to the younger Alberti on how they should manage their business (in the broadest sense) has sometimes been seen as epitomizing the Renaissance merchant's outlook, particularly his description of time as a precious asset that must never be wasted and his injunction always to avoid useless and unnecessary expenses. His maxim, which he ascribes to Benedetto di Nerozzo, that the merchant should 'always have his fingers stained with ink', has justly become famous as an expression of the arch-mercantile credo of one who must always take note.[30]

Such note-taking could relate to everything, from the credits and debits of a bank to the aberrance of a wife. The merchant-patriarch thus emerges as one who records and calculates, who sees and knows, who keeps his counsel and favours secrecy, all motivated by a single aim: control. Giannozzo himself provides the perfect simile for this. He recalls that Benedetto di Nerozzo, in the manner beloved by 'you men of letters', sometimes used the example of ants to demonstrate how we ought to save for the future, and bees to illustrate harmonious social relations. The head of the family, he suggests, could instead be likened to a spider:

> You have seen how the spider arranges the threads of his web in rays, so that each one of them, no matter how long, finds its beginning, its root, its point of origin in the centre, where that most industrious animal dwells. Once it has woven and ordered its work, it dwells there alert and diligent, so that if any of the threads, no matter how minute or distant, is touched, it feels it immediately, rushes there, and takes care of everything. This is what the head of the family should do. Let him study his affairs and arrange them so that they all depend on him, originate with him, and find support in the safest places. Then let him stay there in the centre, vigilant and quick to hear and see everything, and if something should require his attention, let him take care of it immediately. I do not know if you like this similitude of mine, Lionardo?[31]

Lionardo does like it, yet the reader might not find it comforting. Industrious they may be, but spiders are also frightening
to many. They are not social animals but solitary predators.
Any other living thing that enters their web is likely to be
regarded either as an enemy or as prey. Some are venomous.
The simile suggests that the patriarch must construct a world
that is in every way an extension of the self: a web of relations
in which all things have their origin in his will alone. Here,
more than anywhere, Alberti annunciates his understanding
of Giannozzo's *masserizia* as a formidable technique of power
– a set of practices through which power is both produced and
exercised. The technique practised by this figure, who stays 'in
mezzo intento e presto a sentire e vedere il tutto' (in the centre,
vigilant and swift to hear and see everything), is moreover
markedly spatial and visual in character. In this regard, it is
worth remembering that *De pictura* and the third book of *De
família* are essentially contemporary texts. Giannozzo's analogy
is a highly pictorial one, something that is signalled at the start
when he says that the simile will allow him 'to explain more
clearly and almost paint before your eyes' what he is speaking
of. There are also some commonalities between the ways in
which Alberti speaks of a painting and the spider's web, since
he says that both must be woven or stitched together (*tessuto*).
More strikingly, the threads (*cordicine*) of the web are arranged
in rays (*razzi*), a word Alberti uses repeatedly in *De pictura* when
describing the visual rays that are the primary vehicles of sight.
And just as the visual rays converge to form a pyramid, in
which they all meet at a single point in the eye of the spectator,
so in the web all of the rays meet at one point in the centre,
where the spider dwells.

There are thus clear echoes, in the spider-patriarch's network of pure vision and control, of the painter's visual pyramid. But there are also echoes of the perspective grid. Indeed, the spider seems to inhabit the impossible position of the vanishing point itself (or the 'centric point', in Alberti's terms), looking out along orthogonals that now appear divergent, rather than convergent, and that are crossed by transversals that form a set of concentric circles. The spider might therefore seem to stand for the vanishing-point-as-eye considered above, for a form of scopic mastery that is closely bound up with subjectivity and with the knowledge – and in a sense the making – of the self. And just as we saw that Alberti spins the theory of perspective from his own self, which he posits as the only origin, the same is manifestly (literally, in the case of the spider) true here, where everything finds its 'beginning, its root, its point of origin' in the centre, and where the patriarch studies his affairs and 'arranges them so that he alone is the origin of everything', and 'they all depend on him'. If the perspective construction, with its insistence on the author's arbitration, speaks of will to power, then the web of relations does so equally. Both employ geometrical reasoning (and Alberti would have known that a long tradition considered spiders to be natural geometers) to aid in powerful acts of will and imagination: acts aimed ultimately at building and shaping different realities (*istoria* and domestic sphere) according to their own judgements.

The same idea perhaps animates Giannozzo's view that, once a family grows so large that it cannot live under one roof, it should nonetheless exist 'under the shadow of a single will'.[32] Here, however, the appeal is also to adherence to a common interest, an idea that would itself soon prove fanciful, at least at the level of the *consorteria*, when the Alberti's financial collapse occasioned an indecorous scramble for individual advantage rather than any real familial solidarity.[33] Of course, the arachnid order of the spider's web is unachievable, as Lionardo immediately points out. Giannozzo agrees that one cannot in truth see and control everything, and it is for this reason that he taught his wife to look after day-to-day domestic issues according to his own methods, while he attended to grander affairs. To be the head of a family, if the spider simile is anything to go by, must have been an anxious business, demanding a constant, draining vigilance. No wonder Giannozzo dreams of escape to the country, where the web can be policed in a more relaxed fashion. Consideration of his spider simile must also be tempered by his many remarks regarding the bonds of love uniting family members and his fierce loyalty to his clan. What emerges is a strange mixture of familial feeling and individualism, affection and authority, that points towards a fluctuating and unsettled duality at the heart of patriarchal identity.

Alberti was alive to this, as he was to the many other ambivalences and contradictions that the family could sustain. The fourth book of *De familia* explores his interest in another kind of relationship: friendship. This could be less charged, at least theoretically – and there was quite a body of theory to consider. For example, Alberti owned a manuscript copy of Cicero's treatise on friendship, *De amicitia*, which he must have read closely, even if his annoyingly unforthcoming marginal notations do not testify to it.[34] The participants in Alberti's dialogue examine the notion of friendship from different angles, considering its various instrumental and intrinsic goods. Alberti also addressed the topic in other ways, including, as we will see, in the vernacular poetry competition that he organized in Florence, and in works of fiction, where his approach was more elliptical. Among these can be numbered the *Canis*, the funeral oration written for his dog, usually dated between 1438 and 1440. This is another paradoxical encomium and one that is again shot through with autobiographical content; so much so that in some places it reads like a direct parody of the *Vita*, with which it is roughly contemporary. The dog is singled out for its good nature and loyalty, and its preference for prevailing through friendship rather than force.[35] In life, Alberti sustained a number of lasting friendships, including with humanists such as Leonardo Dati and Cristoforo Landino, although relations with some other scholars could be strained. Friendship allowed for a different form of familiarity, one that was complementary to and could also mitigate the disappointments of family life.

BENEDETTO'S PALACE

This is not to say that Alberti ever ceased to be intensely concerned with his family. Members of the Alberti clan appear as speakers in two other dialogues: the short *Cena familiaris* (Family Dinner), which continues some of the themes of the *De familia*, and the *Pontifex*, in which two members of the Alberti family who were both bishops discuss the duties pertaining to their office. That Alberti was one of the first figures we know of to set out his family tree – a document that still survives, drawn in his own hand (illus. 39) – shows how seriously he engaged

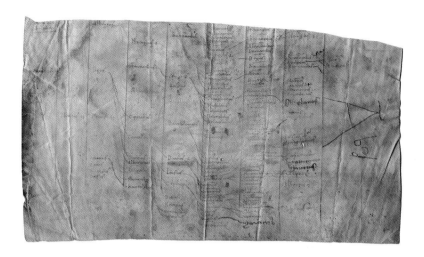

with the topic and how much significance he attributed to his lineage (or rather *patri*lineage, since only the men of the *consorteria* are named – a fact that itself reflects the markedly patrilineal structure of Florence's elite families).[36] The fallout from the unpaid legacy rumbled on long after the two cousins Benedetto and Antonio died (in 1437 and 1445 respectively) and continued to affect not only Alberti's writings but his material circumstances. Ultimately, it seems, it would lead to the unexpected outcome of his inheriting much of the ancestral family home, the palace built by Benedetto di Nerozzo on via de' Benci between the Corso dei Tintori and the Borgo Santa Croce in Florence. In a document of 1468, the notary Marco Parenti, who had assisted Alberti with various matters over the years, set out the legal division of the palace between Alberti and his nephew Bernardo, the son of Antonio di Ricciardo. The division is distinctly uneven, with the lion's share of the spaces going to Alberti and his cousin being left a modest apartment in which to live with his family.

39 Leon Battista Alberti, family tree of the Alberti family, with later additions, on parchment.

Alberti also received a number of properties in Bologna that had previously belonged to his cousin Antonio. This may well have been a friendly arrangement, relieving Bernardo of some of the burdens of maintenance and taxation, while not depriving him permanently of ownership, for Battista, who died four years later, willed his share of the Florentine palace and the Bolognese properties back to Bernardo.[37]

There is some irony and no little justice in this palace finally coming into the hands of one who had been conspicuously excluded, by his father's will, from taking any share of the ancestral properties. There is also some justice to it coming from his cousin Antonio's estate, against which he had for so long sustained a claim. Neither of those relatives, we might speculate, would have been much pleased by the outcome, but for Alberti it must have felt like vindication (not least because inheriting property was traditionally *the* chief marker of belonging to an elite family).[38] It was not that he planned to live there. By that time, he visited Florence only rarely. However, possession of the palace confirmed that he was the true heir to Lorenzo and Benedetto; that he really was an Alberti. Locating him firmly within the circles of both his family and his city, possession of the palace might have represented a homecoming in a profoundly existential sense.

But where, in these last years of his life, was his home? His last vernacular dialogue, *De iciarchia* (On Leadership), opens with Battista making his way down from the church of San Miniato, the Romanesque basilica perched high on a hill above Florence, described by the chronicler Giovanni Villani as 'la grande e nobile chiesa de' marmi' (the great and noble church of the marbles) on account of its polychrome marble facade

40 Master of Saint Cecilia, *Madonna with Child and Angels*, 1313, fresco, Oratorio di Santa Maria delle Grazie, Florence. The oratory has been completely rebuilt.

(see illus. 61).[39] The climb is a steep one (Dante compared it to one of the rugged ascents in Purgatory) and Alberti says that he went there frequently in order to fortify himself both spiritually and physically.[40] He might also have gone there to commune with his ancestors, since San Miniato had benefited significantly from Alberti money, its sacristy richly frescoed with scenes from the life of St Benedict and decked out with expensive wooden furnishings for which Benedetto, exiled from Florence and about to embark on a pilgrimage to Palestine, had provided in his will. In the dialogue, Alberti says that having come down from San Miniato he encountered his friends Niccolò Cerretani and Paolo Niccolini (both based on real people from the civic, mercantile world of Florence) 'while passing over the bridge close to the oratory built there by our Alberti'.[41] The bridge in question must be the Ponte del Rubiconte, which is now known as the Ponte delle Grazie after the oratory of Santa Maria delle Grazie, built over its northernmost abutment in the late fourteenth century by the wealthy merchant Iacopo di Caroccio Alberti. The oratory housed a miraculous image of the Virgin Mary, whose protection was sought especially in relation to flood waters – something that is alluded to in the dialogue, as the characters stand on the bridge and discuss the swollen condition of the river (illus. 40). Alberti seems to have added some paintings of his own to the oratory, which Vasari mentions having seen there and describes in strikingly negative terms.[42] After exchanging some remarks on the bridge, the friends make their way back to Battista's house, presumably the palace that he had recently inherited, and sit down to converse by the fire.

The dialogue thus begins by traversing a highly charged familial topography, starting at San Miniato, moving to the Oratorio di Santa Maria delle Grazie, continuing (almost certainly) along the long thoroughfare of via de' Benci where the Alberti's ancestral dwellings stood, and ending at the very hearth of the palace constructed by his grandfather, the building in which his father Lorenzo had been raised. As the characters discuss the troubling state of the city, with Paolo's son and two of Battista's nephews listening attentively, Battista makes an extraordinary remark. 'I am', he observes of Florence, 'like a foreigner here; I came here rarely and lived here only a little.'[43] This seems like a devastating admission that he had never succeeded in truly integrating into either his city or his family; an acknowledgement of a kind of uncanniness that would not allow him to feel at home even when he was, in a sense, most at home. The sentiment could not be further from the euphoric tone of the letter to Brunelleschi. And yet we must be cautious in interpreting it. It is, after all, the character Battista who speaks, not Alberti himself. Perhaps Alberti was simply not willing to relinquish the authorial distance that he had spun from his sense of familial and civic estrangement. Or perhaps, alongside his poetic melancholia, he wished simply to acknowledge the fact that his life was not centred on Florence. By this time, he was a longstanding resident of Rome and a frequent visitor to the courts of Ferrara, Mantua and Urbino. As such, his attentions were focused on many cities. Indeed, he was increasingly preoccupied with the very idea of the city itself.

SIX

The City

n October 1438 Alberti travelled with the curia to Ferrara. The occasion was a great council, summoned by Pope Eugene IV, to attempt the unification of the Roman Catholic Church of the West with the Greek Orthodox Church of the East: a grand affair that brought dignitaries from far and wide. Located on the Po river in northern Italy, Ferrara was an attractive venue, as it was easily accessible by water from the Adriatic port of Venice. It was also a historically pro-papal city. Indeed, its ruler, the Marquis Niccolò III d'Este, acquired much of his legitimacy from Rome, since he governed his territories as a Papal Vicar (a position also enjoyed by Sigismondo Malatesta prior to his dramatic damnation). Niccolò was, in addition, the *signore* of the city, a title bestowed upon his ancestor Obizzo II d'Este in 1264, and thereafter renewed in a series of communal elections that, by and large, were little more than formalities.[1] While some trappings of communal government remained, including the main advisory council, the Savi, the marquis's grip on power was near-total. Niccolò was a *principe* and Ferrara was a princely city. On the flank of the cathedral, facing the communal palace, the coat of arms of the Este was given equal prominence and displayed side-by-side with that of the *comune*.[2]

41 Pisanello, *Leonello d'Este*, 1441, tempera on panel.

Alberti must have found Ferrara a congenial place, for it was a city where scholars were held in high regard. Niccolò's son Leonello (illus. 41), who succeeded as marquis in 1441, did not just support humanists but actually was one, having been schooled by Guarino da Verona. Leonello seems to have been an adept student, achieving an advanced level of Latin and going on to maintain a lively correspondence with some of the leading thinkers of his day. At Ferrara, he presided over a refined court in which humanistic studies flourished. Such a place could not fail to appeal to Alberti. As has been demonstrated, he methodically courted Este patronage, and by the early 1440s he was a regular (and highly esteemed) visitor to the city.[3] This required considerable skills in the delicate art of courtly behaviour: skills of exactly the kind that Alberti would examine so coolly in the fourth book of the *De familia*. Princely patronage could of course confer status and material reward, and Alberti, like other humanists, sought it for these reasons. Most importantly, however, it afforded further support for his intellectual projects. It also, perhaps, provided new material. Many of Alberti's undertakings involved the investigation of different forms of power; powers that he would dissect, anatomize and force into unstable confrontations with principles drawn from moral philosophy. Ferrara constituted a showcase of princely authority and the ways in which it could enter into a mutually reinforcing relationship with some types of humanism. It also showed how such princely authority might interact with another realm of meaning-making that Alberti had already recognized as a great repository of will to power: the visual arts.

THE ESTE HORSE

Early in his reign, Leonello decided to erect a bronze equestrian statue to his father Niccolò III. It would stand in the city's main piazza, outside the Este palace, facing the cathedral. A competition was held, from which two Florentine artists, Antonio di Cristoforo and Niccolò Baroncelli, emerged as finalists. The Savi struggled to choose between them and concluded that they would require the assistance of 'experts in painting'. Leonello ordered them to consult one and Alberti was called in.[4] It may be that he was summoned as a result of the Marquis's personal recommendation. That, at least, is the impression given by Alberti in *De equo animante*, a treatise on horses which the competition inspired him to write and which he dedicated to Leonello. There, addressing the marquis directly, Alberti recalls his pleasure, as 'one who delights in both painting and sculpture', at having been selected as a 'judge and expert'.[5] Part of that pleasure must have arisen from his observing the rapid success of his bid to establish himself as an authority on art. Another part perhaps derived from his having found in Ferrara the possibility to contribute to civic life in ways that were not available to him in Florence, where he did not enjoy political rights and where he maintained an uneasy relationship with the city's cultural establishment.

The nature of Alberti's judgement regarding the Este monument cannot be precisely determined, but he may well have engineered the competition's final outcome – a compromise in which Niccolò fashioned the horse and Antonio made its rider. These were not the only elements of the work, since they were themselves installed on top of a grand arch, made

42 Copy after Antonio di Cristoforo and Niccolò Baroncelli, monument to Niccolò III d'Este, Ferrara. Supporting arch attributed to Matteo de' Pasti and Niccolò Baroncelli. The original statue was destroyed during the Napoleonic occupation of the city.

from marble in an *all'antica* (antique-style) idiom (illus. 42).
From the outset, this arch seems to have been positioned in
front of the Este palace and was probably always joined to it
at the back. Fluted columns – one free-standing, the other a
half-column, engaged to the building behind it, and both with
ornate 'composite' capitals – support a round arch, above
which a full entablature holds up the base of the statue. The
statue was destroyed during the Napoleonic occupation of
Ferrara but a modern copy provides a good impression of its
appearance. Niccolò is shown as self-possessed and authoritative, with the baton and beret of a leader. With its coffering,
roundels and other classicizing details, the marble structure
below was undoubtedly intended to recall an ancient Roman
triumphal arch (albeit in abbreviated form). We have seen
that a humanist such as Alberti could dignify himself with an
ancient-style biography, and that a patrician such as Giovanni
Rucellai could do the same with an ancient-style facade. In
like fashion, then, a ruler such as Leonello d'Este could enhance
the prestige of his dynasty with an ancient-style memorial.
After all, bronze equestrian monuments had a proud Roman
pedigree, and surviving examples, such as the well-known
statue of the emperor Marcus Aurelius in Rome, could still
be seen.

The extent to which such works influenced the thinking
of the marquis, his artists and his expert judge, Alberti, cannot
be known with certainty. There were many precedents for
equestrian monuments of this kind, although none was exactly
equivalent to it. Funerary statues in northern Italy sometimes
featured an effigy of the deceased on horseback, as did votive
sculptures, including the wax *immagini* that hung in the church

43 Paolo Uccello, *Funerary Monument to Sir John Hawkwood*, 1436, fresco, Cathedral of Santa Maria del Fiore, Florence.

of Santissima Annunziata in Florence.[6] In the same city, Paolo Uccello's fresco commemorating Sir John Hawkwood, a *condottiere* from Essex in England and the leader of Florence's military forces at the end of the fourteenth century, is formally close to the Este monument (illus. 43). The similarity makes sense, since Niccolò III was a *condottiere* too, but the differences are also telling. Hawkwood's cenotaph, which was commissioned in 1436, is in the Duomo. It is not a sculpture but a painting of a sculpture and as such is distanced from the viewer by an extra layer of representation. The potentially seigneurial imagery of a warrior leader seated on his horse – imagery undoubtedly appropriate for the memorialization of a *condottiere* – was thus carefully contained in this republican city. At Ferrara, there was no such equivocation. The statue stood in the open, in the most significant of locations, adjoining the Este palace and returning the gaze of the life-size effigy of Niccolò's father Alberto, installed on the cathedral's facade opposite.

Ferrara was smaller than Florence, and it had a different urban arrangement. In the Tuscan city, the religious, political and commercial centres were all spaced apart, while in Ferrara they were condensed in one place. The communal palace, which housed the law courts and the Podestà, faced on to the southern flank of the cathedral, looking across the city's main piazza where the shoemakers, money-changers and cloth-dealers plied their trades, and where the city's weekly market was held.[7] There were also buildings that had no equivalent in Florence. The aforementioned Este Palace (also known as the Cortevecchia) occupied a dominant position, opposite the cathedral, while just to the north there stood another

Este possession, a great castle known as the Castelvecchio
(illus. 44). This giant fortress was built in response to a tax
riot of 1385 and it constituted both the most visible symbol
and the most effective instrument of Este power in the city.[8]
The Florentine government palace was also sometimes described as a fortress, but the Castelvecchio was different, being
primarily a military building and serving to protect not the
comune but a single family. The Este, then, had good reason to
be preoccupied with architecture, since it provided key support for their rule, and it should come as no surprise that it
was apparently Leonello who suggested to Alberti that he
should consider writing an architectural treatise.[9] Alberti's own
enthusiasm for this project surely stemmed not only from a
desire to produce theoretical accounts of all of the visual arts

44 Castelvecchio, Ferrara. The building has undergone significant
modification.

but from his understanding, gained from the experience of
cities such as Florence and Ferrara, that to write a treatise on
architecture and urbanism was also to conduct an investigation
into politics and the nature of power – matters with which,
as we have seen, he was deeply concerned.

REPUBLICS AND TYRANNIES

De re aedificatoria (On the Art of Building), the lengthy treatise
that Alberti began writing in the 1440s, is a landmark in the
history of architecture and urbanism. We will turn our attention to it more fully in the coming chapters but will touch
here briefly on just a few relevant points. *De re* was a major
work of neo-Latin literature. As such, it cannot have been
aimed primarily at architects (however they might be defined
in this period) but was presumably produced with humanists
and with princes such as Leonello d'Este in mind. Certainly,
political leaders of the later fifteenth century, ranging from
Leonello's successor Borso d'Este in Ferrara to Lorenzo de'
Medici, the de facto ruler of Florence, were keen to get their
hands on it once it became available.[10] At the centre of the
treatise they would have found a discussion of the differences
between cities governed by republican, princely and tyrannical
regimes. Each would appear differently, and Alberti explains
how. As in the other treatises on the arts, he adopts a normative tone and speaks in the first person. He does not examine
how individual cities are in fact, but explores how hypothet-
ical cities ought to be in theory. The result is disconcerting.
Alberti inserts a modest amount of conventional moralizing,
including the expected denunciation of tyranny – a subject

on which there was a substantial body of political theory –
but his discussion often feels strangely unmoored. His survey
of the architectural means appropriate to each regime is cool
and detached (at least outwardly) and shot through with
ambiguity.

He begins by observing that a just prince – that is to say,
one whose position is sanctioned, and whose conduct is governed, by law – will have a palace in the centre of the city,
where he is approachable by all. A tyrant, on the other hand,
will require a fortress, since he governs by force rather than
consent. In these passages, Alberti employs legal definitions
regarding just rulers and tyrants that he would have learnt
during his studies in Bologna. The tyrant would also, he says,
do well to forsake the city centre, as his people are in effect
his enemy and he should not allow himself to be surrounded.
Instead, it would be better for him to site his stronghold by
the city walls. Departing from the realms of the feasible,
Alberti pursues his argument towards its logical extremes,
asserting that the most effective way to dominate a city is to
divide it and suggesting that this might best be achieved by
the construction of a tall, fortified and heavily guarded wall
that would form a circle within a circle. The lower orders – a
category that would certainly include the 'ciompi' (wool
workers) on whose coat-tails Alberti's grandfather Benedetto
had ridden to power in 1378, and perhaps also a good deal of
the *popolo* besides – could be confined to the cramped quar-
ters of the city centre, while the well-to-do would inhabit the
more spacious outer ring. In such a city, the tyrant could rest
easy, knowing that his men occupied all of the vantage points
and that his people would struggle to unite against him.[11]

No ideal city is described in *De re aedificatoria*. Instead we find a kind of inverse parody of Bruni's description of Florence as a series of concentric circles, reimagined by way of Dante's *Inferno*. It is not something that Alberti seriously suggests should be built. Rather, it offers a clear demonstration of architecture's relationship to power. If we feel uneasy, it is perhaps because here we encounter what Manfredo Tafuri has characterized as 'the ethical crossroads implied by the techne of modernity': the recognition of the will to power inherent in humanist-architectural discourse and the entirely open potential for that power's use.[12] Alberti does not hide this reality from us and nor does he seek to relieve our anxiety. Indeed, he destabilizes our position further when he swiftly breaks down the fragile distinction that he has only just established between the prince and the tyrant. Although the former will reside in a palace, he will nonetheless require a fortress to be on the safe side. The tyrant, on the other hand, will dwell in his fortress

45 Castel Sismondo, Rimini, 1437–44.

but will still need a palace for entertainment.[13] Ultimately, each will have recourse to similar, if not identical, means. Perhaps they are different; perhaps they are the same.

Looking over these passages, a well-travelled Renaissance reader could reflect on the cities they knew and decide where they stood in relation to Alberti's discourse. The Marquis of Ferrara, we have seen, inhabited a palace sited towards the city centre. On the other hand, he had a fortress standing hard by to protect against any repeat of the uprising of 1385. In Rimini, Sigismondo Malatesta was similarly motivated by a revolt to construct a huge stronghold adjoining the city walls, a building that he apparently designed at least partly himself and for which he also enlisted the expertise of Brunelleschi (illus. 45). Closely bound to his personal identity, the fortress appears on the reverse of a medal showing Sigismondo's portrait, just as the Tempio Malatestiano does in another instance (illus. 46). The sculptor was the same Matteo de' Pasti who fashioned a bronze image of Alberti, with the winged eye staring out on the other side. Sigismondo's stronghold was surrounded by walls and a moat, with tall towers that faced not outwards towards some external enemy, but inwards towards the city itself. The sense of a siege-engine turned towards the

46 Matteo de' Pasti, medal showing Sigismondo Pandolfo Malatesta (obverse) and Castel Sismondo (reverse), 1446, bronze.

47 Agostino di Duccio, *Cancer*, c. 1455, marble, Chapel of the Planets
(Chapel of St Jerome), Tempio Malatestiano.

walled circuit of Rimini is strongly conveyed in a sculpted relief in the Tempio Malatestiano, attributed to Agostino di Duccio. Located in a chapel decorated with the signs of the zodiac, it shows Cancer, Sigismondo's own star sign, as a huge crab suspended above Rimini, with the Malatesta fortress seen at the top of the city (illus. 47). There is a striking sympathy between the polygonal castle and the heavily armoured creature, both of which seem to be bearing down on the city below. The prince/tyrant, or tyrant/prince, it reminds us, must, like the patriarch, exert total control over his domain. But where the latter, as a spider, relies mostly on wiles and calculation, the former can also avail himself of the full military might embodied by the crab.

PERSPECTIVE ON THE CITY

Elsewhere, Alberti conducted a different, and thoroughly moral, discourse regarding the city-states. Upon the death of Niccolò III in 1441, he sent to Leonello a work of moral philosophy, the *Theogenius*, which he intended to have a consolatory function. How much consolation the marquis would have drawn from it is, however, debatable. The dialogue is divided into two books in which characters with allegorical names (a technique used also in the *Philodoxeos* and some of the *Intercenales*) discuss moral themes. In the first book, Microtiro (First Beginner) goes to see his friend Teogenio (Divinely Inspired), seeking consolation at a moment of ill fortune. Teogenio tells him about an occasion when he was conversing with Genipatro (Father of the People) and they were approached by the young, rich and arrogant Tichipedo (Child of Fortune), who was then in his pomp but has since, we learn, fallen on hard times.[14] Teogenio recounts the conversation that ensued, in which Genipatro explained to Tichipedo that all of his good fortune was worth nothing and that even those in the most abject condition were happier and better off than him. Despite some initial attempts to refute Genipatro, Tichipedo is ultimately overwhelmed by the devastating force of the older man's argument, and by the end of their conversation he is almost in tears.

This is perhaps a sort of vindication fantasy on the part of Alberti, who makes the target of his discourse listen and react in a way that no spoiled rich kid would in real life. In the second book, Teogenio speaks in his own voice in a long diatribe against the foolishness and presumption of human beings. The themes are familiar to Stoic philosophy and, insofar as they stress the fickleness of fortune and the necessity of cultivating virtue, they are also characteristic of Alberti's writings as a whole. However, one cannot help but be struck by the force of Alberti's pessimism, which hangs heavy over every page. For sure, there are some pleasures allowed to human beings: being in nature, reading and scholarship, friendship, and the cultivation of *virtù*. But, particularly in the second book, we learn that the ordinary run of things is suffering, though should that seem hard to bear we should understand that the true cause of that suffering is almost always our own folly. The dialogue closes with Teogenio explaining that death is to be welcomed rather than feared, even if suicide should not be contemplated. Hardly an uplifting note.

To some extent, *Theogenius* does perform the functions of a traditional *consolatio*, reminding us that others have it worse than we do, and that it is within our power to reduce our suffering by following reason and moderating our expectations and desires. At the same time, the dialogue also addresses another topic: the nature of the republic (or state) and the meaning of citizenship. It does so by moving outside of and establishing a vantage upon the city. At the outset, Microtiro climbs up a steep path to find Teogenio in the woods. Genipatro, we learn, lives even higher up, further into the forest. It was in the woods that Tichipedo came crashing through, hunting with his many retainers, and ran into the two sages. Everything, in other words, takes place outside of the city. Teogenio and Genipatro are exiles of long standing. Even Tichipedo has, since his exchange with Genipatro, been forced from his *patria*. Throughout there is a suggestion that the city impedes clear moral reflection, while natural settings facilitate it. Or rather, being outside of the city allows for perspective and thereby clears the way for a certain sort of philosophical investigation. This is why the 'writer saints', to use Jarzombek's term, are to be found in the woods. In this light, it could legitimately be argued that the tone of the dialogue is anti-urban. It is not, however, anti-civic, or at least not straightforwardly so.

In fact, Genipatro asserts that participation in government is a worthwhile activity – but more often in theory than in practice. This is because the mob of people always prefers a rascal. It is hard for good men to achieve anything in the republic, since the crowd will hate and persecute them for their very goodness. For this reason, Genipatro does not mind his exile. He continues to love his *patria*, and says that he tries to help it through his scholarly activities. In fact, he claims that he is no less a citizen for not living in the city, arguing that 'it is first and foremost unwavering affection for the *patria*, not the fact of living there, that makes me a true citizen [*vero cittadino*]'. This is manifestly the case, he argues, since otherwise any time a good citizen went outside of the city walls, their citizenship would cease, while any barbarous enemy who entered would immediately become a citizen. Moreover, he *is* present, he says, 'in the temples, in the theatres, and in the houses of the foremost citizens, where good people frequently both read and speak of me and my works'.[15] Just like painting, then, writing can make the absent present.

This seems to assert a particular claim about authorship and citizenship. In the *Vita*, Alberti had elaborated on the difficulties that he first faced when writing in Tuscan, since he had not grown up with the language. With hard work, however, he soon improved, becoming so adept that 'some of his fellow citizens who wished to be thought eloquent in the Senate confessed that at times they had adorned their speeches by borrowing elegant turns of phrase from his writings'.[16] In other words, Alberti found, as a writer, an indirect means to contribute to the proceedings in Florence's government palace, despite enjoying no political rights in the city. In fact, Genipatro's positions point to a Petrarchan conception of writing as an activity that demands a special form of citizenship that excludes physical presence in the city. Petrarch had referred to himself, poetically, as a 'citizen of the woods' and there is clearly some echo of that idea in the sages of the *Theogenius*.[17] At the same time, their situation recalls a real category of citizenship – that of 'sylvan citizens' ('cives sylvestres'), who enjoyed rights of citizenship while being relieved of the obligation to live in the city.[18]

There are some significant differences, not least that
Genipatro and Teogenio are exiles without political rights,
while sylvan citizens were generally rich countrymen. However, perched as they are on a wooded hill not far from the
city, the sages are not exiles in the standard sense, as the
Alberti had been. Instead, their position stands for a kind of
exemplary 'outside-ness' from which the nature of their true
'inside-ness' might be debated. Genipatro's remarks seem
deliberately to disregard the highly developed legal frame-
works that governed matters such as citizenship and exile,
and instead to appeal to natural law – something that is
entirely consistent with Alberti's own approach to legal matters, outlined in his short treatise *De iure* (On the Law), which
he composed in 1437. There, specifically identifying himself
as one who had devoted his life to philosophy rather than
jurisprudence, Alberti argues strongly for the supremacy of
natural law over man-made codes. In so doing, he opens the
way for a form of belonging to both the family and the city
that the legal formulas thoroughly excluded.

PROFUGIORUM AB ERUMNA

None of this is to say that philosophizing can occur only in
the country. In the early 1440s Alberti completed another
moral dialogue, *Profugiorum ab erumna* (On Avoiding Mental
Anguish), in which the locations are entirely urban. The first
book is set in the cathedral of Florence. In the second, the
characters take a walk around the city. In the third, they go
back to the cathedral and stand outside of it. Once again, the
discourse is consolatory, with Agnolo Pandolfini attempting

to counsel Niccola di Vieri de' Medici, who is experiencing that broadest and most profound of early modern mental maladies, melancholia. This condition, which ranges from a feeling of general unease through to anxiety and depression, has in Niccola's case been triggered by a period of adverse fortune. In response, Agnolo deploys the full range of Stoic remedies – something that should not surprise us, since Alberti took the Stoic philosopher Seneca as one of his primary models. Indeed, *Profugiorum* sometimes circulated in Florence under the vernacular title *Della tranquillità dell'animo*, making clear reference to Seneca's own text on the tranquillity of the soul, *De tranquillitate animi*. However, matters do not rest there. Niccola is not fully convinced of the efficacy of the Stoic doctrines, and Agnolo goes on to explore a much broader range of approaches, some grounded in philosophical texts and others deriving from experience. Everything from taking walks, to talking with friends, to sex and moderate drinking is considered. Ultimately, the reader is left with the sense that no permanent resolution is possible. Mental tranquillity will for everyone remain a work in progress that must be supported by good habits of mind, including humour.[19]

Undoubtedly, the urban setting of *Profugiorum* is significant. Although there is no physical description of the city itself, it must nonetheless be understood as providing the great theatre of experience within which this wide-ranging discussion of the human condition takes place. The sense of immersion within this everyday world, entirely of human facture, seems to be connected to the tenor of the conversation, which is in some ways more nuanced than in *Theogenius*. In the latter case, the feeling of pessimism, sometimes articulated through the enumeration of various species of ill fortune and disaster, can feel overwhelming. *Profugiorum*, by contrast, is more varied, and also takes a more complex view of human nature. Simulation and dissimulation are considered in some depth, as the characters explore the moral consequences and advantages of pretence – something that Agnolo judges to be on occasion a necessary strategy for protecting the self and achieving one's aims. In doing so, he evokes as an exemplar Ulysses (the Romanized form of Odysseus), who in the final episodes of the *Odyssey* must pass as a beggar in his own home, enduring all manner of insults and ill treatment, so that he may finally unmask himself, defeat the suitors who would steal away his wife and reclaim his birth right.[20] It is an interesting choice, since Ulysses was not a straightforward character. Famous for cunning, he was praised by Petrarch but condemned to one of the lowest circles of hell by Dante as a deceiver. In *Profugiorum*, this multiform figure – spinner of tales, strategist, hero and sometime wandering exile – becomes the emblem of a pervasive moral restlessness inherent in human life. Homer, in fact, is alluded to with some regularity in the text, which, although written in the *volgare*, is full of allusions to Greek and Latin literature. Indeed, with its inclusion of the mosaic simile that we examined in Chapter Two, the *Profugiorum* is characterized by a deep preoccupation with meaning, and the means of its making and communication. Itself a mosaic of many tesserae, the text is built upon an implicit process of continual translation from Latin and Greek into the vernacular, as well as a transition back and forth between figurative language and plain speaking, artful fiction and apparent fact, irony and sincerity.

The siting of so much of the dialogue in and around the cathedral is not casual. The first book opens with praise of the building, which Agnolo frames in terms that, as Christine Smith has shown, are highly reminiscent of rhetorical theory: a fluid movement between text and architecture that helps prepare the ground for the mosaic simile at the start of Book Three.[21] As we have observed in earlier chapters, the cathedral seems to have constituted for Alberti a centre of meaning, which he connected closely to his own return from exile in his letter to Brunelleschi. *Profugiorum*, with its complex layers of allusion and its multilingual foundations, is itself deeply concerned with the making of meaning. Throughout, it explores the tension between the drive towards wholeness on the one hand and the acceptance of fragmentation on the other, revealing meaning to be as precarious as the mental and spiritual balance sought by the characters. That Alberti considered the cathedral a particularly appropriate place for such speculations seems to be borne out by his staging there of a very singular poetry contest on 22 October 1441, not long before he composed the *Profugiorum*. Called the *Certame coronario* (the contest for the crown), participants were asked to present poems on the theme of friendship, composed in an antique style but using the vernacular. A poem that was long believed to have been made by Alberti for the occasion, though not officially entered in the competition, still survives.[22] In fact, it seems likely that it was written by his friend Leonardo Dati, but in any case it attests to the two men's shared intellectual interests. Penned using an ingenious combination of ancient and modern metres, incorporating hexameters for the first time in the *volgare*, it constitutes an extraordinary hybrid, being neither entirely of antiquity nor of its own age. Instead it appears strangely untimely, and in that sense – some might think – unmistakably contemporary.

Writing in this manner and organizing the *Certame* were not neutral acts. In the mid-1430s, when Alberti was still new to the city, a vigorous debate had erupted among the Florentine humanists regarding the status of the *volgare* and its relation to Latin. Some considered that Latin had always been an elite, written language even in ancient Rome, arguing that it had not evolved haphazardly but had been consciously constructed by intellectuals according to rational principles (making it the product of an *ars*, just as Alberti claimed for painting). No doubt, such humanists reasoned, the Romans had possessed a vernacular of their own, but they had brought Latin to such a degree of polish that it was the only form suitable for serious literature. Others conjectured that, on the contrary, Latin had been the only language of the Romans, not artificial but natural, and used both for writing and for everyday speech. According to this view, it was in fact Rome's vernacular, and this indicated that the humanists, rather than pursuing only Latin eloquence, should also aim to refine their own tongue, just as the Romans had done.

A formal dispute was held before Pope Eugene IV at Santa Maria Novella in Florence in March 1435, sharply dividing opinion among scholars who understood that the matter went to the very heart of their intellectual practices.[23] Straight away, Alberti took sides. The preface to Book III of *De familia* reveals him as a passionate defender of the vernacular. Probably around the same time, he wrote a grammar book of the Tuscan language, setting out to demonstrate that it was not some irregular word-salad fit only for the unlearned but was structured according to grammatical rules, just as Latin was.[24] His introductory remarks to the work take a defensive tone, anticipating the attacks of his opponents, and opposition was indeed likely because the debate was of such great import. This might seem strange to a modern observer – a case of scholars blowing something trivial out of all proportion and entangling themselves in intricacies of little interest to the wider world. In many ways, however, the argument was crucial. Implicated within it were the accessibility of learning, the status of imitation, the relationship of the modern to the ancient world, the shape of history and the very possibility of progress.

The *Certame* was a bold move in this debate. In part, it must have been born from Alberti's desire to extend humanism beyond the restricted circle of humanists and into the civic realm of the Florentine republic. In a deft act of fundraising, he managed to persuade Piero de' Medici to put up the money, but even so the event failed. Alberti had assembled a panel of expert judges, drawn from his colleagues in the papal curia and other members of the Florentine humanist elite. One can only imagine the excitement that he must have felt as he stood at the centre-point of his newly regained *patria*, listening to the fruits of his efforts to orchestrate a greater refinement of his ancestral language, and seeming to effect, in the presence of his scholarly peers, a remarkable fusion of Latin and vernacular culture. The judges, however, were not having it. After hearing all of the offerings, which included poems by a kinsman of Alberti, the banker Francesco d'Altobianco, as well as his close friend, the humanist and churchman Leonardo Dati, who he perhaps hoped would win the prize, the panel decided that none of the poems merited the crown.[25] Instead, they decreed that it should be awarded to the cathedral's treasury. Perhaps they felt it was a convenient way to avoid favouring any one contender above another. Or perhaps they had little sympathy for Alberti's project. Maybe they were irked by his polemical assertion of views that grated with some of their most deeply cherished beliefs. Alberti, certainly, understood it as an insult. He penned an energetic protestation in which he accused the judges of snobbish arrogance, asking why they had agreed to participate in the first place if they held the idea in such contempt.[26] The argument seems also to have spilled beyond the page and into the piazza. A letter from Leonardo Bruni, the most prestigious of all the judges, suggests that Alberti had accosted him in public in the days that followed.

This correspondence points to the existence of genuine tensions. Bruni himself professed no disdain for the vernacular, and he accepted that it was in theory capable of expressing everything that Latin could, but he did not agree that Latin had been a spoken language in antiquity, and he favoured its use in the present as by far the most polished tongue available. Perhaps the tensions sprang also from other sources. Bruni, who possessed a formidable intellect and was a master of both Latin and Greek, was at the time the chancellor of Florence as well as one of the foremost intellectuals in Europe. In many ways, he was the model of what has later come to be known as a 'civic' humanist: a scholar who was also a political operator and who placed his eloquence at the service of the state. Alberti, of course, spent his life in the employ of the pope and courted the patronage of other princes, but he was fundamentally attracted to the notion that the author must position himself as an outsider. Already in the *De commodis* he had noted the compromises with power that civic humanism entailed, and he had made his own scepticism manifest. Taking recourse to his standard accusation against detractors, he now suggested that the next *Certame* should be dedicated to the theme of envy. Bruni, in a letter to Alberti's friend Dati, responded archly that stupidity might be more appropriate.[27] In fact, there was to be no further contest. Whether, ultimately, this was owing to the hostility of influential humanists or to Alberti's preoccupation with other projects, the *Certame* remained a one-off event, standing as a peculiar mixture of success and failure, revival and innovation. To some extent, it smacks of the duality that had always characterized Alberti's relationship with the scholarly establishment, showing him as eager to impress and ingratiate on the one hand, and to polemicize and stand apart on the other. The episode also encapsulates his desire to find meaning in the city and to make it into a site of cultural recovery. That venture had not fared especially well in Florence, where the *De pictura* was met with near total silence in Alberti's lifetime and where the outcome of the *Certame* must have seemed like a stinging public rejection. Nonetheless, Alberti would continue with his projects. His efforts, however, would be directed elsewhere, and they would take on new forms.

SEVEN

Technology and Folly

lberti made his most lasting home in Rome, in the parish of Santi Celso e Giuliano, in the *quartiere* (district) de' Banchi.[1] As its name would suggest, the area was frequented by bankers, who included many Florentines among their number. Fronting onto the River Tiber, it looked across the water towards the Castel Sant' Angelo, the vast structure built as a mausoleum of the emperor Hadrian and subsequently converted into a giant fortress to defend the papal regime (illus. 48). Beyond this was the walled area of the Borgo and the Vatican. Whenever he left his house, Alberti would have had ample opportunity to mull over the meaning of these architectural defences, whose great expansion under Pope Nicholas V he would have witnessed at close range, and to consider whether his papal employer more closely resembled a tyrant or a prince. In his broader travels around the city, meanwhile, he could have inspected many ancient ruins: temples, aqueducts, theatres, triumphal arches and more. From large, well-preserved structures, such as the Pantheon and the Colosseum, to small tombs and broken sections of wall, there was much to see. Too much, almost. To assimilate the sprawling, multi-layered and deeply complex city of Rome was a daunting task that might arouse

48 Castel Sant'Angelo, Rome, constructed 135–9 CE as the mausoleum of Hadrian and subsequently converted into a fortress.

both intense exhilaration at just how much survived and deep melancholy regarding all that had been lost. In this vein, Alberti's humanist friend and colleague Poggio Bracciolini opened his 1447 dialogue on the vicissitudes of fortune on the Capitoline Hill, marvelling at the ruins of the once great city and lamenting the disappearance of many of its physical structures.[2] Seeking out inscriptions among the undergrowth, he went on to reconstruct as much as he could piece together.

Another of Alberti's friends, Flavio Biondo, had already completed a magnificent treatise on the topography of the ancient city, entitled *Roma instaurata* (Rome Restored), and was busy at work on the follow-up, *Italia illustrata* (Italy Illuminated), which would take in the whole of ancient Italy. In that book, he compared his work as a historian, sifting through the fragments of the past, to that of one who attempts to salvage a shipwreck by reassembling those of its pieces that might still be found. It is appropriate then that it was at Biondo's recommendation that Cardinal Prospero Colonna asked Alberti to undertake an unusual feat of underwater archaeology involving the attempted recovery of a real boat.[3] The ship in question was a pleasure barge, one of two that lay on the bottom of Lake Nemi, around 30 kilometres (20 mi.) from Rome. Both were large, over 70 metres (230 ft) in length, and both had been made in the first century CE for the mad emperor Caligula. At least one of them originally supported a large building, which had once been equipped for lavish entertainments. The lake occupies a dramatic position in a volcanic crater, surrounded by a thickly wooded ridge (illus. 49). It is wild, craggy country; the sort of Roman *campagna* that would later be so beloved of painters such as Salvator Rosa and that feels as though it is possessed of mysterious, primal forces. And indeed, strange cults had arisen there, including the rituals attached to the Temple of Diana Nemorensis, where, in ancient times, one could only accede to the office of priest by murdering the previous incumbent.[4] For centuries, the ships had lain on the bottom of the lake, known of by medieval fisherman and presumably forming both a foreboding and a tantalizing prospect for those looking down upon the dark waters from the small town of Nemi, perched on the ridge high above. At Colonna's behest, one of the boats was now to be raised to the surface – a spectacular resurrection that would bring the antiquarians of the fifteenth century face to face with an extraordinary fragment of the Roman world.

One can see why Alberti appeared the right man for the job. He possessed all of the requisite cultural learning, while also commanding mathematical competence and technical knowledge. In his treatise on painting, he had demonstrated considerable acquaintance with geometry. He had served as an expert judge for the commission of the Este horse, and he was now at work on a major treatise on the art of building. Raising the ships was nonetheless a new challenge, and a daunting one. He succeeded, but only very partially. Employing specialist Genoese divers to attach ropes, and erecting a lifting mechanism on a floating platform of wine barrels, he was able to effect some movement. The ancient fabric, however, could not withstand the strain and broke apart, so that only the ship's prow came to the surface. This Alberti examined closely. He briefly describes the materials in his architectural treatise, remarking on the pine and cypress woods, the lead sheets, the fabric soaked in black pitch and the copper nails – presumably

actually bronze nails, which Biondo also mentions – used by the Roman shipwrights.[5] No doubt Alberti went into more detail in his short treatise *Navis* (On the Ship). We can only speculate about its contents, however, since the work is lost. Ultimately, then, the pickings were slim, but that did not mean that the enterprise had failed completely. For one thing, it had provided a grand spectacle. In fact, the entire papal curia had travelled to Nemi to witness the event. No ship had emerged, but something had come out of the water and those present had received a brief, alluring glimpse of the secrets hidden on the lake's floor.

FUN WITH MATHS

It was Alberti's understanding of mathematics that caused Biondo to recommend him to Colonna. This is an area that Alberti had engaged with at least since his student days. Some indication of his proficiency can be gained from a work that he wrote for Meliaduse d'Este, the brother of Leonello,

49 Lake Nemi.

around the middle of the century (and certainly before Meliaduse's death in 1452). Titled *Ex ludis rerum mathematicarum* (The Mathematical Games), it is a short text written in the vernacular, setting out a series of problems in practical mathematics. Many of these are to do with measurement, detailing such things as how to establish the heights of towers, the

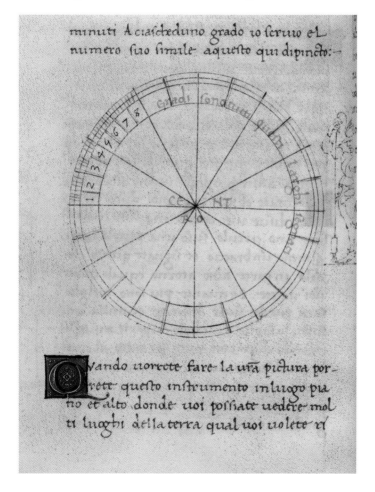

50 Diagram of sighting disc, illustration from Leon Battista Alberti, *Ex ludis rerum mathematicarum* (The Mathematical Games).

depths of waters, the distances between points both near and far, and the area of a field. In addition, Alberti sets out how to tell the time by the stars, how to make a gravity-powered fountain, how to measure the speed of a ship and many other things besides.

Mathematical problems they might be, but they are designed to be fun. Alberti thus took pains to write them down in a clear and simple fashion, while also emphasizing that he had left out much of the complicated mathematics that underpins them. Meliaduse, whose father Niccolò III had forced him to pursue a career in the Church rather than take the reins of power in Ferrara, had received an excellent human-ist education at the hands of the Sicilian scholar Giovanni Aurispa, but he was no mathematician. The first seven games proposed by Alberti, and particularly those concerned with measuring the heights of towers, rely on Euclid's principles regarding similar triangles, which had also played an impor-tant role in *De pictura*. Indeed, there is a distinctly optical aspect to many of these tasks, with Alberti promising to show how they can be accomplished by sight alone ('col veder').[6] Unusually, he included illustrations so that Meliaduse could see exactly what he meant. What they looked like we cannot know, since although there are drawings in the existing manu-scripts, these vary considerably from one version to another and contain several basic errors, so that it is unlikely that they closely resemble Alberti's originals.[7] Clearly, however, he felt that some visual assistance was necessary.

Meliaduse might have been a churchman but he was also part of a princely family, and the problems that Alberti details are especially fitting for a high-ranking member of a ruling

house. Many of them are concerned with assessing urban and
rural territory, including such activities as measuring the height
of a tower at the end of a piazza, gauging the width of a river
and determining the distances between cities. All such practices relate to the possession of places and all of them could
clearly also have military applications, as Alberti acknowledges
when explaining the method for levelling a bombard. As so
often, then, the relationship between knowledge, power and
the creative imagination is at play within the text. This is
apparent, for example, in the way that Alberti moves from a
discussion of war to one about the making of pictures. Having
explained how to position artillery, he says, 'I should add to the
things said above a certain instrument very suitable, as you
will think, for these requirements, and especially for those
using the trebuchet and similar machines of war. But I use it
for very pleasurable things, such as how to measure the site of
a town, or the picture of a city, as I did when I depicted Rome.'[8]

The reference here is to one of his most influential technical achievements: a coordinate map of the city of Rome in
which he attempted to determine the precise position of the
city's major monuments, topographical features and walls.
The procedure to derive the coordinates is described in *Ex
ludis rerum mathematicarum*. It involves sighting with a plumb line
across a disc whose perimeter is divided into 48 degrees, each
of which is further subdivided into four minutes (illus. 50).
You must take readings of the positions of everything you see,
and then repeat the process from other vantage points, making
sure that you align your disc properly with the places that you
have already taken readings from. Making a little pointer out
of paper, centred on a disc whose perimeter is subdivided in

the same way as the disc that you used for sighting, you can draw lines on a sheet of paper corresponding to the degrees and minutes that you noted down. You start with the readings taken from the first point and then move on to the second. Crucially, you can fix that second point *anywhere* along the line that you have drawn leading to it from the first point, without having to know the real distance between them. From the second point, you again draw lines corresponding to the degrees and minutes that you observed. Where the lines taken from two sightings intersect, you can establish a coordinate, and this itself allows you to move on to the sightings from other points and establish still more coordinates based on two or more sightings. In this way, you can plot on a piece of paper the relative position of the major features of a city, without measuring any distances and only relying on angles.

It seems barely credible that such a procedure could work. Yet it does, and very precisely (at least in theory, since in practice some degree of error is likely to creep in during the sighting process). What guarantees its functioning is again the Euclidian principle of similar triangles: that is, the principle that such triangles are identical in everything but size and are thus strictly proportional to each other.[9] The same principle was fundamental to *De pictura*, where it ensured that the painted image could correspond proportionally to things seen. In the *Mathematical Games*, it allows for the accurate determination of relative position. Of course, if the 'player' wanted to go beyond position and know the real distances that are involved, it would be enough to measure between two points and extrapolate the rest from there – and Alberti has a method for that too.

Whether or not he developed it specifically for the purpose, it was perhaps inevitable that Alberti should apply this coordinate mapping to Rome, the city in which he lived and which the humanists strove unendingly to recover. This is attested to not only in the *Mathematical Games* but in a short work entitled *Descriptio urbis Romae* (The Delineation of the City of Rome). There, Alberti begins by explaining that

> using mathematical instruments, I have recorded as carefully as I could the passage and *lineamenta* of the walls, the river, and the streets of the city of Rome, as well as the sites and locations of the temples, public works, gates, and commemorative monuments, and the outlines of hills, not to mention the area which is occupied by habitable buildings, all as we know them to be in our time.[10]

Presumably, this 'recording' was carried out according to the method outlined in the *Mathematical Games*. The results are presented to the reader in a series of tables containing coordinates. The *Descriptio* explains how these coordinates might be used to draw an accurate map that would, by and large, correspond to the map that Alberti himself must have made when he undertook his survey. In order to do it, one needs a piece of paper on which to draw a circle whose perimeter you must, as before, divide into 48 degrees, with each degree subdivided into four minutes. This is the circle in which the image of the city will be contained, and Alberti calls it the 'horizon'. One must then fashion a 'radius', or spoke, that extends from the centre to the edge of the circle and that swings around like a clock hand. The length of the spoke should be divided into 50 degrees, each one again comprising four minutes. For every coordinate, Alberti provides a number relating to both the spoke and the perimeter. He also provides some basic indication of what type of coordinate it is, so that for long objects such as the city walls, the reader will know when they encounter a corner or the apex of a curve. All that remains is to plot the coordinates and join them together with lines.

What Alberti has in fact done here is to produce a transmissible, reproduceable, digital image, long before what Walter Benjamin would later term 'the age of mechanical reproduction'. The *Descriptio* is, as Mario Carpo and Francesco Furlan neatly put it, 'the encryption of a picture in a digital file transmitted with all instructions necessary to recreate a new picture proportionally identical to the archetype, but in the absence of the original drawing'.[11] For Alberti did not accompany the text with an image of his own map – something that would undoubtedly have been distorted at the hands of copyists, just as occurred with the *Mathematical Games* – but instead rendered that map within the text as an alpha-numerical code. Thus what at first sight seems meagre and dry, being just a few pages of Latin writing followed by tables of numbers, turns out to be the key to something visually rich and deeply engaging: the whole of the city of Rome, set out before the viewer in miniature, and done so with dependable precision.

Such precision was, of course, essential to Alberti's enterprise, but as always it was precision of a particular kind. The map is a picture, but not of the city as it appears to our sight. When he drew it, Alberti placed the Capitoline Hill at the centre. Perhaps, like Poggio, he conceived of it as the natural vantage from which to contemplate Rome, and it is indeed the most central of the city's hills. Looking from its highest point, Alberti would have been able to see far in every direction. He did not, however, produce an image of that panorama. Although the coordinates are derived by optical means, the map seeks to avoid visual distortions and only in the most abstract sense does it adopt a point of view. It is not perspectival, but instead seeks to show things 'as they are', or perhaps more accurately 'where they are'. It thus constitutes knowledge of a particular kind, presenting itself to us as mathematical rather than perceptual. It vaunts an internal consistency that allows it to act as an *analogon* for the city itself. It is therefore quite distinct, in its appearance, from the kind of *pictura* described in the treatise on painting, eschewing not only perspective but colour and relief. Both types of image, however, share important structural similarities. Like the coordinate map, the perspectival picture is also a measurable image, and both of them are rooted in the notion of proportion.[12] Yet the *Descriptio* includes no element of *istoria*, and is more purely technical and mathematical in character. In this way, it might have reassured some observers, suggesting that cities are things that can be made knowable by measurement and brought under control. Alberti, however, knew differently.

THE VIEW FROM ABOVE

Back in the realms of moral philosophy – Alberti's most familiar ground – cities and the people they contained were as problematic as ever. A different type of view from above appears in one of the *Intercenales*, entitled *Discord*. Here, Mercury

and Argos meet at Fiesole, high on one of the hills overlooking
the city of Florence. Argos, who, being covered all over with
eyes, is an apt figure for the author himself, has been charged
with finding the goddess Justice, who has disappeared from
the world. Mercury asks him how the search has progressed
and Argos says that he thought he might find the goddess in
Florence, attracted there by its sumptuous dwellings. However, there is no trace of her, and in fact nobody on earth has
ever seen her, except for a few old men in Rome 'who repeat
a tale which their grandfathers had heard from their great
grandfathers. They allege that Justice used to lodge in their
city, which, though large and ancient, is now quite ruined and
deserted.'[13] The vista of Rome, then, when looked at with a
moral gaze, appeared very different from when it was viewed
mathematically. In the story, the gods are in fact searching for
Justice to help them settle a controversy. Many of the male
gods are claiming to be the father of the goddess Discord,
since they reckon her to be the most powerful deity of all.
Jupiter himself asserts that he fathered Discord with Justice
and so the goddess has been called to testify. Yet, as we learn,
there is no justice on earth.

The idea of two gods standing at a high place where they
can look down on terrestrial cities and find mankind wanting
perhaps derived from a dialogue of Lucian, in which a similarly
themed but longer discussion takes place between Hermes
and Charon. Lucian was also an important influence for
another work in which Alberti decried the moral condition
of mankind far more extensively: a novel-length piece of Latin
prose fiction entitled Momus. Variously dated to the 1440s
and the 1450s, Momus is perhaps Alberti's greatest literary

achievement. Indeed, it must rank among the most significant works of fiction to have emerged from the entire Italian Renaissance. The eponymous antihero is the god of harsh criticism and mockery, whose fall, rise and fall again provides the structure around which the narrative revolves. Having offended the other gods, Momus is condemned to harsh punishment but flees before it can be enacted. Falling from the heavens and landing on the earth, he stirs up so much trouble as an exile among human beings that the gods decide it would be preferable to return him to his former position, where they can keep an eye on him. Armed with the techniques of simulation and dissimulation, which he has learned from men, Momus prospers as a courtier, but he continues to cause strife, persuading Jupiter that the earth ought to be destroyed and made again from scratch – something that Jupiter agrees to despite not knowing how to accomplish it. All manner of chaos ensues and Momus seems set to achieve his revenge on both mankind and the gods, both of which he loathes equally. However, he cannot maintain his dissimulation and he is eventually condemned for a second time, castrated and chained for all eternity to a rock in the ocean.

Momus is a highly satirical work, and the targets of that satire are numerous: gods, men, the well-to-do, the lower orders, architects, philosophers, heroes and women, to name only some of them. Above all, however, it sets its sights on the figure of the ruler, and the work in fact circulated for a long time with the subtitle *On the Prince*. While the prince is to be understood here in a universal, abstract sense, scholars have been in little doubt that Alberti also set out specifically to critique his own employer, the pope, although *which* pope he had in mind is harder to determine. Could it be Eugene IV, unable to command his own territories and driven from Rome for the best part of a decade? Or is it more likely his successor, Nicholas V, who launched ambitious plans to rebuild large areas of Rome and who sought to assert papal supremacy within the Church, aggregating immense power to himself? Recent opinion has tended to favour the latter, not least because Jupiter's architectural overreach finds a number of parallels with Nicholas's own ambitions for his city. Since the nineteenth century, it had been widely held that Alberti himself was Nicholas's architectural advisor for these projects. However, the hypothesis formed by Manfredo Tafuri at the end of the last century, that Alberti was not a central but a marginal figure at court, and that he wrote the *Momus* as a dissimulated critique of a ruler whose building programme was entirely at odds with his own architectural thinking, has steadily gained ground.[14] The reality, of course, may be messier and less clear cut, as reality is wont to be. Jupiter perhaps contains aspects of both Eugene and Nicholas – and maybe also other rulers that Alberti had encountered. It is also possible that Alberti did have some degree of involvement in Nicholas's schemes, even if he was for the most part an estranged critic.[15] The sheer force of his attack and the many echoes of the Nicholine pontificate in the world that he creates are, however, undeniable.

Momus also, in common with other Albertian texts, contains a number of autobiographical elements. In the final book, Alberti tells the story of Gelastus, the shade of a dead philosopher, who accompanies Charon, the ferryman to the underworld, on a strange sightseeing trip to the earth. When, on the return journey, they meet Momus in the midst of the ocean, Gelastus recounts a life story, including exile and familial estrangement, that is instantly recognizable as Alberti's own. In other cases, the authorial self seems to be projected into altogether more strange and distorted images. For example, Momus's daughter Fame (or Rumour), whom he fathers when he rapes the goddess Praise, is covered in eyes, as well as darting tongues and ears, and flies all around the world at incredible speed. 'Moreover', Alberti tells us, 'there is nothing so private, hidden and wrapped in shadow that the goddess Fame, burning with lust to see, hear, and tell, does not instantly try to search out, identify, and divulge to common view, with the utmost diligence, astounding watchfulness and unbearable toil.'[16]

There are distinct echoes here of the fly, and while that creature might be considered a comic take on the winged eye, this one is monstrous and grotesque. Momus himself, as an exile and outsider, perhaps contains touches of the author, even if he is far too negative a character to be considered in any sense a figure for Alberti. Contemporary humanists suspected there might be a real person behind Momus's mask, and Francesco Filelfo – who had been chased out of a cushy university position at Florence by his Medici enemies – wondered if it might be based on him. However, Momus is not so easy to pin down. For, as Alberti tells us right at the outset, despite all the variety of the world 'you would still not find among either men or gods anyone *so* extraordinary, *so* naturally perverse, *so* multifariously unlike anyone else as one of the gods whose name is Momus.'[17] The character is too multiform to be mapped precisely onto any one model. He does not bear much resemblance to the god of the same name who appears in some of the dialogues of Lucian. If anything, as Christine Smith has suggested, he is closer to a sort of classically dressed-up antichrist or Satan.[18]

Nonetheless, just as Fame mixes truth with falsehood, Momus occasionally cuts his malice with a little benevolence. He produces a sober text on rulership and gives it to Jupiter, though the king of the gods immediately casts it aside and forgets it. He also offers some words of caution regarding the remaking of the world; words that echo, or perhaps parody, some of Alberti's own remarks in *De re aedificatoria*. And in fact, the visual arts are never far from the discussion. Towards the end of the story, Alberti makes much play on the difference between things themselves and their representations when the gods decide temporarily to switch places with their own man-made statues – a decision that leads to catastrophe. Grandiose architecture is criticized through a number of examples, from the splendid triumphal arch erected at the behest of Juno by the architect Arugine (Rusty), which swiftly collapses under its own weight, to a great theatre built by human beings in order to propitiate the gods – something that Charon judges to be an absurd waste of time and money and not nearly as beautiful as a single flower. There is talk of the inferiority of modern architects when compared with the architects of old who built the world, but it is also suggested that it would make more sense to seek advice from architects rather than philosophers, since it is the former who are truly wise.

When it comes to understanding human nature, however, one must turn to the painters – at least if we are to believe an anecdote told to Gelastus by Charon. The passage is undoubtedly among the most significant that Alberti ever wrote.

It occurs at a point when Charon has reached the peak of his frustration with Gelastus' philosophy, which he condemns as empty, verbose wordplay. Finally, he says that he, a ferryman, will teach the philosopher to 'know thyself' (a reference to the famous injunction that was, in ancient times, inscribed at the Temple of Apollo at Delphi). The story he relates was told to him, he emphasizes, not by a philosopher but by a painter, a man who 'by himself . . . saw more while looking at lines [*linea-menta*] than all you philosophers do when you're measuring and investigating the heavens'. What follows is a strange version of the creation and fall of man. Charon explains that the creator of the world first fashioned human beings from clay. Using moulds, he wrought both men and women, making the latter from any of the former that turned out defective (a characteristic touch of Albertian misogyny), and he created all of the animals in the same way. Having thus crafted human beings, he pointed out to them his own dwelling, high up on a hill, and said that they should make their way there. Once they arrived, they would enjoy all manner of good things. However, they should not stray from the path that he indicated, which would be steep and difficult at first but would soon become easier. He also said that, since they were all made from the same clay, any humans who were dissatisfied with their form could change themselves into the shapes of other animals if they so pleased.

After this, the humans started to climb. Straight away, some decided to transform themselves, preferring, due to their own folly, 'to look like cattle, asses, and other quadrupeds'. Others, spurred by their desires, strayed from the path as they passed through settlements along the way, and soon found themselves lost:

There, in steep echoing valleys, impeded by thorns
and brambles, faced by impassable places, they turned
themselves into assorted monsters, and when they
returned to the main road, their friends rejected them
because of their ugliness. Consequently, realising that
they were all made of the same clay, they put on masks
fashioned to look like other people's faces. This artificial method of looking like human beings became
so commonly employed that you could scarcely distinguish the fake faces from the real ones, unless you
happened to look closely at the eye holes of the masks
that covered them. Only then would observers encounter the varied faces of the monsters. These masks, called
'fictions', lasted until they reached the waters of the
River Acheron and no further, for when they entered
the river they were dissolved in its steaming vapour.
So nobody reached the other bank unless he was naked
and stripped of his mask.[19]

This dark and disturbing tale suggests that many humans
are in fact monsters who pass among us by means of dissimulation. It implies that much, but not all, of humanity is fallen,
but unlike many Christian doctrines it describes no process
of redemption. The wearing of masks is a recurrent theme
throughout *Momus*, and indeed the title character becomes
most adept at it, at least for a while. Alberti himself was, fig-
uratively speaking, a consummate mask-wearer, beginning with
his very first work when he adopted the guise of Lepidus.
When Momus exalts in the power of dissimulation – 'Oh,
what an excellent thing it is to know how to cover and cloak

one's true feelings with a painted facade of artificiality and studied pretence!' – his exaltation seems, to some extent, to be Alberti's own.[20] And yet in Charon's dark fable, humanity's masking is simply monstrous. Gelastus is shaken by the story, asking Charon, 'are you making this up as a game, or are you telling the truth?' The question seems to be placed on behalf of the reader, who is never sure, in *Momus*, where the joke ends and seriousness begins. The reply is far from comforting: '"No," said Charon. "In fact, I plaited this rope from the beards and eyebrows of the masks, and I caulked my boat using their clay."'

This answer conjures, in markedly violent and abject terms, the spectacle of a brutal destruction of humanity's pretences. It perhaps also points towards Alberti's preoccupation with simulation and dissimulation as being concerned more with unmasking than with masking itself.[21] For the truly striking thing about his adoption of Lepidus as an alter ego and *nom de plume* is arguably not so much his taking up of the mask when he wrote the *Philodoxeos* as his putting it down again years later when he reissued the play. It is as though he wished to say to the entire community of humanists: 'Behold! This world of antique letters is really a thing of our own facture!' In the commentary, Alberti seems to present his act of masking as a necessary tactic to achieve a broader unmasking; in the narrowest sense an unmasking of envious critics, and in the broader sense a laying bare of the operation of authorship and the internal workings of the humanism that he so cherished. In such revelatory acts he perhaps sought to demystify the nature of cultural production.

Within many of Alberti's activities, there is a tension between this impulse to 'lay bare' and a quite different drive to construct and to solve problems. He delighted in new techniques and technologies and fervently embraced progress. In this vein he proposed new methods of mapping and surveying, undertook the raising of sunken ships, and, in a short treatise on sculpture, invented a method for deriving the measurements of statues and individuals using an instrument very similar to the one he speaks of in the *Descriptio*. Towards the end of his life he also expressed enthusiasm for the printing press, an invention that would soon thoroughly revolutionize the practice of scholarship.[22] He did so in a treatise on ciphers, in which he set out a method for making and then unscrambling a code using a rotating circle – something that might be seen as a development of his method of making and transmitting the picture of the city of Rome, which also involved a kind of coding and decoding.

In all such undertakings, Alberti distinguished himself from many of his humanist contemporaries by his willingness to enter into technical discourses and by his interest in doing and making. Indeed, in the *Vita* he claims that 'from craftsmen, architects, shipbuilders, and even from cobblers and tailors, he tried to learn, wishing to acquire any rare and secret knowledge contained in their particular arts'.[23] Whatever the truth of that remark, Alberti certainly did diverge from the usual run of scholars by foraying so deeply into technical territory. In a sense, one might say that he sought another way to investigate the world around him by drawing a series of interrogatory circles: around the individual, in his treatise on sculpture; the family, in the patriarch's web; and the city, in the *Mathematical Games* and the *Delineation of the City of Rome* (and we might note the similarity between the spider's web and the implied circular grid of the *Descriptio*). The treatise on ciphers, meanwhile, describes a sort of hermeneutic circle.

At the same time, however, Alberti's moral writing maintains a relentless scepticism about humankind's ability truly to improve its lot. Over and over again, he seeks to expose the baseness and squalor of human life. Even the good must suffer mental turmoil for which there is no definitive answer, as we discover in the *Profugiorum*. In *Momus*, Alberti perhaps sought to draw a very different kind of circle to the ones that he made in the technical works, a circle that we might characterize as enclosing existence itself. For here too we meet with a horizon, but where, in the *Delineation of the City of Rome* the horizon is the boundary that supports the making of place and the determination of position, in *Momus* it is the horizon of the world, described as 'that point by the edge of the seashore where the sea, the land and the air separate'; a point that is 'cut off from place'.[24] It is this boundary that Charon and Gelastus cross when they leave Hades and step into the world above, coming, as it were, from behind the picture, passing through the vanishing point and entering the great *istoria* of human life. But in *Momus*, there is little meaning to be found inside the circle of the horizon, only folly, while outside is death. And yet this tragic and unsparing view cohabits in Alberti's outlook with a strong belief in the value of constructive action, a belief that is nowhere more in evidence than in a work dating from the same period as *Momus*: the treatise on architecture.

EIGHT

Architecture

t least since 1436, when he had written his letter to Brunelleschi, Alberti had nurtured an interest in architecture. Scattered throughout his writings we find architectural metaphors, references to real and imagined temples, and various reflections on the built environment. In a striking passage of the *Profugiorum* Agnolo says that when he is kept awake by pressing cares he sometimes occupies himself by designing great, fantastical buildings in his mind. As the 1440s went on, Alberti began to engage with architecture more directly. Exactly how this new orientation came about is difficult to know. In one sense, it was a natural topic for him to take up, allowing him to complete a sort of trilogy on the visual arts. At the same time, as we have already seen, Alberti was well aware that to write about architecture and urbanism was also to write about politics. This was a subject of intense interest to him but one so highly charged that he seems to have struggled to approach it head on. To understand just how fraught the issue was, one need only reflect on the fact that *Momus* is in some sense a political text, and consider what a multiform and dissimulated piece of writing that is. Alberti's architectural treatise allowed him to explore politics further while also developing his aesthetic

51 Palazzo Rucellai, corner view.

theories and examining many aspects of society and the built environment.

De re aedificatoria, we know, was begun at the behest of Leonello d'Este. It was completed to some degree by 1452, when Alberti presented the text to Nicholas V. It is likely that he continued to work on it for some time afterwards, and possibly for the rest of his life. Undoubtedly, he was deeply influenced by an ancient model, *De architectura* of Vitruvius, an architect and military engineer who had probably served under Julius Caesar and who presented the emperor Octavian (Augustus) with a treatise on architecture in the late first century CE. Vitruvius' work had survived the collapse of the ancient world in fragmentary form, and a fuller and less corrupted version of the text was unearthed by Poggio in 1414. Alberti learned much from Vitruvius, even adopting his ancient predecessor's division of his treatise into ten books. However, the nature of his discourse was fundamentally different. Vitruvius sought in large part to transmit the time-honoured ways of building handed down from the Greek tradition, including a range of canonical building types and their measurements. Alberti had another objective. As Françoise Choay has argued, he sought nothing less than to produce generative rules for the entire built domain, fashioning a discourse that did not simply show how to make a number of specific buildings but that aimed to provide the fundamental principles for the making of *any* building.[1] Throughout the treatise, Alberti's erudition is everywhere to be seen, and many ancient authorities are invoked to support his positions. As with *De pictura*, however, he speaks in the first person, selecting, judging and choosing between the views of others, while also referring to his own experience, always retaining full command of the discussion and never submitting to a higher authority. This treatise on architecture was the first to be written in the Renaissance, but it was also markedly different from anything surviving from antiquity. In the judgement of one contemporary scholar of the subject, it is 'probably the most important and consequential text ever written on architecture'.[2]

In a prologue to the work, Alberti extolls the virtues of architecture, commenting on its exceptional range, usefulness and power to affect all persons and every aspect of life. He also offers a definition of the architect, emphasizing:

> it is no carpenter that I would have you compare to the greatest exponents of other disciplines: the carpenter is but an instrument in the hands of the architect. Him I consider architect, who by sure and wonderful reason and method, knows both how to devise through his own mind and energy, and to realise by construction, what- ever can be most beautifully fitted out for the noble deeds of man, by the movement of weights and the join- ing and massing of bodies. To do this he must have an understanding and knowledge of all the highest and most noble disciplines. This then is the architect.[3]

Undoubtedly, there is polemical intent here. Alberti gives the word 'architect' a sense that it had only ever hazily, incon- sistently and intermittently enjoyed during the Middle Ages, using it to denote someone who does not engage in manual work but whose activity is purely projective and founded upon knowledge of the liberal arts.[4] As with the painter in *De pictura*, he seems to propose a type of practitioner quite unlike most of those who were actually engaged with the design and construction of buildings in the fifteenth century. And as with *De pictura*, his intention must have been both to dignify the art that he wrote about, according to the intellectual hierarchies of the time, and to claim for himself a particular status as the expositor of that elevated discipline. In doing so, he helped to usher in the modern conception of the architect that, for better or for worse, remains influential to this day. Alberti's distinction between the architect and the manual labourer is reinforced towards the end of the prologue when he tells us that a building is a body (*corpus*), by which he means a physical entity, and that, like all bodies, it consists 'of lineaments and matter, the one the product of thought [*ingenium*], the other of Nature; the one requiring the mind and power of reason [*mentem cogitationemque*], the other dependent on preparation and selection; but we realised that neither on its own would suffice without the hand of the skilled workman to fashion the material according to lineaments.'[5] Architects, then, are concerned with lineaments, which are produced by their thought, and with materials, which they must select and consider how to use, although it is the craftsman who will ultimately fashion them. Alberti begins with the former.

Lineaments – *lineamenta* in Latin – form the subject of the first book of the treatise. They consist, Alberti tells us, of lines and angles. 'All the intent and purpose of lineaments lies in finding the correct, infallible way of joining and fitting together those lines and angles which define and enclose the surfaces of the building.' As such, they determine 'the whole form and appearance of the building', yet they have nothing to do with matter, since, while they can appear in material things, they can also exist in the mind alone. 'Since that is the case, let lineaments be the precise and correct outline, conceived in the mind, made up of lines and angles, and perfected in the learned intellect and imagination.'[6] Lineaments, then, determine shape, and they can be worked out and examined mentally – just like geometry, of which they are in fact part. Architecture thus begins with rational projection in the mind, establishing lineaments that can then be instantiated in various ways: in drawings, in wooden models and ultimately in buildings.[7] Arguing that architecture first arose from the need for safety and shelter, Alberti goes on to identify six basic elements upon which all buildings rely: locality, *area* (by which he means the precise plot on which the building has its footprint), compartition (the division of the building into parts), walls, roofs and openings. He proceeds to examine them in order, considering the kinds of lineaments that apply in each case.

All of the six elements of architecture, and especially those such as roofs and openings, should, Alberti says, be considered above all in relation to three principles:

> that is, their individual parts should be well suited to the task [*usum*] for which they were designed and, above all, should be very commodious; as regards strength [*firmitatem*] and endurance, they should be sound, firm, and quite permanent; yet in terms of grace and elegance [*gratiam et amoenitatem*], they should be groomed, ordered, garlanded, as it were, in their every part.[8]

This echoes Vitruvius' well-known maxim that architects must attend to *firmitas* (solidity), *utilitas* (utility) and *venustas* (grace and charm). Broadly speaking, Alberti concentrates more on solidity and utility in the first half of the treatise, before turning to beauty and ornament in the second. Thus Book Two addresses the subject of materials – timber, stone, bricks, lime and sand – from which, as we have seen, the architect must select according to detailed knowledge. Book Three considers construction, which is in some senses also a matter of lineaments, since it depends upon 'the ordered skilful composition of various materials' into an 'integral and unified structure', such that 'the parts it contains are not . . . separated or displaced', and so that 'their every line joins and matches'.[9] Starting with foundations and footings, he moves steadily upwards to consider walls, panelling, bonds and roofs (including vaults), before coming back down to earth to end, as in the mosaic simile in the *Profugiorum*, with the pavement. Book Four turns to public works, discussing cities as a whole, then walls, gates, bridges, drains and harbours.

The structure is thus quite systematic, although it begins to waver in the fifth book, on the works of individuals, which takes in a very large range of building types. Even when the treatise is at its most ordered, however, it does not necessarily seem so to the reader, since the text ranges broadly over many different topics and sometimes feels compendious or encyclopaedic (and indeed medieval encyclopaedias were a key source of architectural knowledge at the time). There is a great deal of erudition on display, with many references to ancient writers, although these were not the only authorities to which Alberti turned for information. In fact, he tells us in the second book that as well as consulting the likes of Theophrastus, Aristotle, Cato, Varro, Pliny and Vitruvius, he depended on his own observations of ancient buildings, as well as wisdom gleaned directly from skilled practitioners. Sometimes these were of more use than the authors, as in the case of pavements, where, having related everything that Pliny and Vitruvius have to say on the subject, he comments that he learnt far more from inspecting buildings himself than he did from any book.[10] All of this results in a work of extraordinary breadth and depth, touching on many topics: political theory; the nature of the city-states; moral anxiety regarding opulence and excessive size or zeal; nature (which Alberti thinks should never be opposed or contested); the relationship between the city and the country; and much more.

BEAUTY AND ORNAMENT

In addition to this, Alberti's treatise, with its discussion of temples, theatres and basilicas, is also an investigation into a lost urban antiquity, and into both ancient architecture and aesthetics. These aspects are especially to the fore in the second half of the treatise, which begins with Book Six, 'On Ornament'. Alberti starts by recapping what he has covered so far and reflecting on his original reasons for undertaking the work. 'I grieved', he says, 'that so many works of such brilliant writers had been destroyed by the hostility of time and of man, and that almost the sole survivor from this vast shipwreck is Vitruvius, an author of unquestioned experience, though one whose writings have been so corrupted by time that there are many omissions and many shortcomings.' As we have seen, shipwreck was sometimes employed by humanist writers as a metaphor for the destruction of ancient culture. In this case, the loss of meaning implied by such a catastrophe is heightened by the nature of its one survivor, Vitruvius, since Alberti complains that 'what he handed down was in any case not refined, and his speech such that the Latins might think that he wanted to appear a Greek, while the Greeks would think that he babbled Latin. However, his very text is evidence that he wrote neither Latin nor Greek, so that as far as we are concerned he might just as well have not written at all, rather than write something that we cannot understand.'[11] Vitruvius, Alberti suggests, is largely incomprehensible. His own task would thus be to restore clarity and meaning to the theory of architecture. In this way, Alberti declares his independence from the foremost authority on his subject and substitutes another authority in his place. For even though texts were lacking, he was still able to learn a great deal from the ruins of ancient buildings themselves. 'I never stopped exploring, considering and measuring everything,' he says, 'and comparing the information through line drawings, until I grasped and understood fully what each had to contribute in terms of ingenuity or skill.' It is on this basis that he proceeds to his subject. Observing that he has already dealt with stability and usefulness, he says that he must now address the matter of charm and delight: 'the noblest and most necessary of all'.[12]

Both ornament and beauty, he asserts, are of incalculable value. Everybody feels their effects, and without them all of our most treasured social institutions would appear base and shabby. Such is the force of beauty that it can even calm a raging enemy and save a building from destruction. But what exactly is this almost magical property and how is it to be distinguished from ornament? The question is unavoidable, yet Alberti is reluctant to address it. 'The precise nature of beauty and ornament,' he warns, 'and the difference between them, the mind could perhaps visualize more clearly than my words could explain.' To provide a definition of beauty is a tall order for anyone, and Alberti resorts to a pre-existing formula in order to do so. 'Beauty', he says, 'is that reasoned harmony of the parts within a body, so that nothing may be added, taken away, or altered but for the worse.'[13]

This notion of aiming to create something that cannot be added to or subtracted from except to the detriment of the whole is one that Alberti had already touched on in the prologue, in Book Two and again in Book Four, where, offering it as a definition of perfection, he attributes the maxim to Socrates. In fact, it seems rather to derive from Aristotle's *Nicomachean Ethics*, a text that was available in a high-quality, up-to-the-minute translation by Leonardo Bruni.[14] There the philosopher suggests that whenever anybody makes something, they naturally seek precisely this balance in which nothing may be changed except for the worse. Beyond this, Alberti's definition also recalls the four most fundamental operations of rhetoric, which Quintilian describes as addition, omission, substitution and transposition, all of which he associates with barbarisms and with solecism.[15] In addition, Alberti's maxim has a testamentary quality and might be associated with the idea of a 'rule' as a guiding principle for an entire form of life. St Francis had ended his own testament with the injunction: 'The minister general, the other ministers and the custodians, through obedience, must add or subtract nothing to these words. Let them always have this text attached to the Rule. When they read the Rule they will also read these words.'[16] In fact, a papal bull issued just four years after the saint's death had allowed the Franciscans to ignore this part of the testament, as Alberti, a trained canon lawyer and himself a drafter of papal bulls, would undoubtedly have known; a state of affairs that might have suggested to him quite how much it was necessary to guard against change.

Regardless of its origins, his definition (or, more accurately, theory) is a clever one. It seems to provide a genuine answer to the question 'what is beauty?' even as it in fact begs it. For, if the definition is to be of any use, we must know how to judge what is better and what is worse, and that is a far more complex proposition. In fact, it is not clear that Alberti considers beauty to be fully achievable in his own terms, since he immediately comments on the difficulty of the task, and observes that 'rarely is it granted, even to nature herself, to produce anything that is entirely complete and perfect in every respect.' All buildings will probably contain some deficiencies, and these, he says, can be remedied with ornament, which he compares to the use of cosmetics by human beings: a procedure whereby the attractive may be enhanced and the ugly hidden. 'If this is conceded, ornament may be defined as a form of auxiliary light and complement to beauty. From this it follows, I believe, that beauty is some inherent property, to be found suffused all through the body of that which may be called beautiful; whereas ornament, rather than being inherent, has the character of something attached and additional.'[17] The distinction seems quite sharp, although perhaps not so sharp as it first appears. In fact, the words that Alberti uses here indicate that ornament is not only 'attached to' but 'com-pacted with' the building, suggesting that it is not always as extraneous as we might otherwise imagine.[18] Nonetheless, it is clear that beauty takes pride of place. Being more abstract, however, Alberti puts off further discussion of it until the ninth book and turns instead to the more practical issue of ornament.

The remainder of Book Six is devoted to ornament in a general sense, while Book Seven discusses ornament to sacred buildings, Book Eight to public secular buildings, and Book Nine to private buildings. Throughout these pages, the archi-tecture that Alberti describes in the first part of the treatise is brought to life, as he seeks to reassemble the full range of ancient ornament, from wall revetment to columns (which he calls the main ornament of architecture), to the ornamen-tation of cities with fora and streets. The reader can be in no doubt that Alberti describes ancient building types made in an *all'antica* style, with columns conforming to what would later be termed 'orders', round arches, entablatures and pediments. Today this is sometimes called 'classical' architecture and there is a tendency to think of it as being 'opposed' to medieval gothic. However, while the beginnings of such opposition can be found in the Renaissance, it post-dates Alberti. He has nothing derogatory to say about the gothic and nor does he identify it as a separate style. He mildly disparages pointed arches, but his only praise of a modern building occurs at the start of the *Profugiorum* where he has Agnolo Pandolfini express his delight at the gothic cathedral of Florence.[19] Indeed, Alberti is far from dogmatic regarding the subject of ornament. He willingly passes on precepts and measurements derived from

his usual sources but he also favours experimentation, innovation and invention.

What he does insist on, however, is the importance of
building syntax, or measurable placement.[20] Thus he says that
great care must be taken 'to ensure that even the minutest
elements are so arranged in their level, alignment, number,
shape, and appearance, that right matches left, top matches
bottom, adjacent matches adjacent, and equal matches equal'.[21]
This brings us back to beauty, which for Alberti consists in the
relationship between parts and the whole. Indeed, while his
definition of beauty might be linked to some specific sources,
and Aristotle in particular, more generally his thinking can
be located squarely within the mainstream of a centuries-old
tradition of aesthetic thought. This is what the Polish philosopher Władysław Tatarkiewicz called the 'Great Theory' of
beauty; the dominant theory of aesthetics that prevailed from
antiquity, through the Middle Ages, into the Renaissance,
and in fact all the way until its eventual overthrow at the
hands of Romanticism. The theory exists in almost limitless
permutations, but all of them assert, in one way or another,
that 'beauty consists in the proportions of the parts, more
precisely in the proportions and arrangement of the parts,
or, still more precisely, in the size, equality, and number of
the parts and their interrelationships.'[22] It thus enshrines the
classical preoccupation with the whole and with the question of how composite objects might truly constitute a single
entity. To this philosophical question, which would later be
classified under the heading of mereology (the study of parts
and wholes), ancient architects had proposed proportion and
measurable placement as the solution. This idea speaks loudly

throughout Vitruvius' treatise, and in that sense Alberti and Vitruvius are at one.

To explain how such a condition might be achieved in an actual building, Alberti introduces another triad of terms, urging architects to pay close attention to outline, position and number as a means of ensuring consistency throughout the building. If all of this is done correctly, it should give rise to the most prized quality of all: *concinnitas*. The term, which is difficult adequately to translate, has attracted much attention from scholars, who have noted its origins in the works of Cicero and other ancient writers. We might describe it as an ideal balance or a harmonic relationship between parts and whole, but such a definition falls far short of its true range. For Alberti says that *concinnitas* is not only the quality through which 'beauty shines full face' but also 'the fundamental rule of nature'.[23] As such, it is not narrowly aesthetic, in the sense that we might think of aesthetics today. Rather, 'it runs through man's entire life and government.' It is clear from this that *concinnitas* enjoys an exceptional status within Alberti's thought, and he asserts that it is the ultimate goal of the entire art of building. Of course, a concept that is so fundamental to the whole life of human beings must necessarily also bear upon the field of ethics. The association of the beautiful with the good was an old one, fully entrenched within the Great Theory, and it is worth observing, in this regard, that the passage of Aristotle's *Nicomachean Ethics* from which Alberti took his definition of beauty is in fact a discussion of virtue, which Alberti considered to be the ultimate aim of all ethical thought and action.

That *concinnitas* is to be found also throughout nature alerts us to another aspect of Alberti's thinking. While nature is sometimes characterized as harsh and oppositional in *De re*, it is at other times treated as a normative force from which the architect should always take his cues. In this regard, Alberti continues to reason as a Stoic, implicitly adopting the imperative that one should 'follow nature' at all times; and indeed both Alberti and the Stoics belonged to a long pre-Cartesian tradition of thought in which human beings conceived of themselves as part of nature and made from the same elements. In another sense, Alberti also clearly seeks to naturalize his own discourse, presenting it as something that is not arbitrary or invented but grounded in nature and as such found rather than made. Again, such preoccupations are inherited from Vitruvius, who is keen to assert that the principles he conveys are beyond dispute – an idea that also lurks in the background of the notion of achieving a condition in which nothing may be changed except for the worse. However, Alberti's naturalism works in more than one direction at a time. In *Momus*, written alongside *De re*, Charon is vocal about the inferiority of architecture when compared to nature, arguing that the great theatre cannot match a single, ordinary flower in beauty.[24] In doing so, he uses language that Alberti seems to echo when he discusses beauty in Book VI of the architectural treatise. Scholars have also noted that Alberti's framing of the division between beauty and ornament contains a certain ambivalence. His comparison of ornament to make-up, something that was often decried by moralists – including Alberti in the *De famiglia* and the *Momus* – perhaps introduces a degree of uncertainty.[25] Ornament, Alberti says, is a complement to beauty, to which it adds lustre. At the same time, it might point to the instability or even the unachievability of the flawless and timeless order from which beauty arises. Such a reading sees Alberti subtly but pointedly loosening one of the wheel bearings of the aesthetic juggernaut of the Great Theory.[26] Here, as elsewhere, he seems to linger on the tension between a compositional procedure leading to a fully realized system of meaning on the one hand, and his own recognition of contingency and the constant undoing of meaning on the other.

CONTINGENCY AND TIME

Some scholars have, rightly, seen Alberti as troubled by the force of time and keen to place architecture outside of its workings. This might account for his insistence that buildings should be made quickly, on the basis of precise plans from which there should be no deviation – something that does not accord with much building practice at the time and that has been associated with a literary or authorial view of architecture introduced by a figure who was, after all, a writer at heart.[27] Alberti would well have known that some buildings that he admired, such as the cathedral of Florence, could not claim any single author and were not worked out in their every detail before they were begun. Of course, he may not primarily have had in mind such vast cathedrals when he wrote about architecture in general terms. They were, after all, highly exceptional buildings, and it may be that he thought more of smaller projects where patrons and architects might aspire to greater control. The Oratorio di Santa Maria delle Grazie, which features at the start of the *De iciarchia*, is a good example. Alberti's ancestor Iacopo di Caroccio left instructions for the completion of this fourteenth-century structure, in which he insisted that it should be built strictly in accordance with the wooden model, or, in the event that the model was somehow destroyed, according to detailed written instructions left with a notary. This might in turn suggest that Alberti's viewpoint here is closer to that of a patron than an architect, while also reminding us of the testamentary nature of his injunctions regarding the introduction of changes to designs.[28] In any case, when Alberti began to engage with architectural design, he revealed himself to be a contextualist of the first order, keen to incorporate history into his works and to set it in dialogue with the sort of building syntax that occupies such a prominent place in his architectural treatise.

The Tempio Malatestiano (encountered in Chapter Four) is a good example of this. In the conversion of this gothic building, he had no choice but to reckon with history, since the original fabric had to be preserved. His strategy was not to downplay the encounter with the past but to emphasize it. As we have seen, Alberti had recourse to an ancient local model when he designed the facade, basing his engaged semicolumns (though not their capitals) on those of the Arch of Augustus, which still stands in Rimini today. Further references to triumphal arches in Rome must have appeared appropriate at the time, since Sigismondo was to be buried within the building, making the facade a prelude to his tomb and allowing it to be understood as a monument to his victories and perhaps his triumph over death. Along the flank, however, we encounter another fragment of the past, though this time it is not so ancient. The round arched openings that incorporate the tombs also reveal the windows of the recently

fashioned chapels with their pointed gothic arches (illus. 52).
Not only does their style contrast with the new exterior but
their placing is at variance with their surroundings, since they
obey a different formal logic, corresponding to the interior;
something that made it impossible for Alberti, once he had

52 Side arch of Tempio Malatestiano, containing earlier gothic window.

settled upon his scheme, to position them in the centre of
each of the bays in which they appear. We are thus presented
with a clash between two different syntaxes, or, at the very
least, a highly syncopated rhythm – one that seems to contra-
vene Alberti's stipulations regarding mathematical placement
in De re aedificatoria. Despite that, it appears not so much as
something that the architect has been forced simply to put up
with, but rather as something that he has (quite literally)
framed and put on display for our contemplation.

Rhythm is certainly a legitimate consideration, and one
that cannot have been far from Alberti's mind. In a famous
letter to one of the on-site architects, Matteo de' Pasti, Alberti
had stressed that he should stick to the dimensions given

53 Letter from Leon Battista Alberti to Matteo de' Pasti, 18 November
1454.

in the model, saying, 'regarding the measurements and proportions of the piers, you can see from whence they are born; any changes that you make will put all of that music into discord' (illus. 53).[29] This coheres with his positions in the architectural treatise, where he asserts that 'the very same numbers that cause sounds to have that *concinnitas*, pleasing to the ears, can also fill the eyes and mind with wondrous delight. From musicians, therefore, who have already examined such numbers thoroughly, or from those objects in which Nature has displayed some evident and noble quality, the whole method of outlining is derived.'[30] For Alberti, natural and architectural beauty, as well as harmonious music, all shared the same *concinnitas*, deriving from numerical relationships. It thus makes complete sense to speak of an architectural composition as 'music' since its harmonic structure will be fully analogous.

This suggests that something highly complex is going on at the Tempio. On the one hand, Alberti aimed to create on the facade the kind of timeless and immutable perfection that he associated with beauty, an order that he sought to naturalize, in his treatise, through comparison with both nature and music. On the other hand, he took pains to present the encounter of different temporalities, and even the encounter between his own architectural ordering and that of the pre-existing fabric of the church, the latter of which was certainly not to his taste, since he urged Matteo, in the same letter, that the facade should be an entirely separate structure 'because I find the widths and height of those chapels disturbing'. The coexistence of these diverse architectural regimes leads to uncertainty over whether Alberti's own ordering is truly timeless, natural and found or whether it is contingent, of its moment and made. The question is rendered more pressing by the handling of some of the architectural elements. To take just one example, we are to understand the entablature, on the facade, as 'supported' – if not literally then at least according to a certain architectural logic – by the semi-columns beneath it. However, that entablature continues along the long flank of the building where no such supports are to be found. Something similar occurs on triumphal arches, but there the flanks are so short that we do not feel the need of support. At the Tempio, however, the sides are longer than the front, and, as the entablature runs right along them, we understand that it does not need to be held up, even notionally – something that in turn reveals the semi-columns to be 'mere' ornament, contributing nothing at all to structural integrity.[31] This might itself cause us to view the facade as an object that is neither natural nor inevitable, but rather a kind of imitation, in some senses as akin to an image as it is to a tectonic structure. Suddenly, we are not so sure where we stand.

All of this might make us think back to Alberti's preoccupation with the mask and wonder whether it is not at work here also.[32] For just as its architect once wore the mask of Lepidus, so the building also seems to adopt an antique persona: something that it does not hide from us but instead announces frankly. The same might be said of the elegant facade of the Palazzo Rucellai (discussed in Chapter Five), which turns around the corner but runs only a short distance, seeming consciously to announce that it is a shallow layer that has been applied, rather than an integral part of the building (illus. 51). The drafted masonry that gives the palace so much of its character also disturbs our sense of the integrity of its individual elements. This is partly because the shafts of the pilasters are themselves drafted in the same manner as the stonework that surrounds them and they project forward only slightly in front of the rest of the bay. They are not made from distinct slabs of their own but are carved from the same blocks as the adjoining rustication. We are thus made to ponder their 'reality', wondering whether we should conceive of them as privileged individual elements that stand in front of everything else, or simply as one more part of a complicated, essentially graphic composition.[33]

Along the bottom of the building, serving as a back rest for the benches and also as a base for the whole facade, is carved a diamond pattern (illus. 54), reminiscent of Roman

54 Palazzo Rucellai, detail of decoration resembling *opus reticulatum*.

opus reticulatum, a method for reinforcing concrete whereby long pyramidal wedges of stone are inserted into the walls with their bases appearing as diamond shapes on the outside (illus. 55). Anybody who spends substantial periods of time among Roman ruins will be familiar with its appearance, although for the most part it is only on display because the stucco or stone revetment that once covered it has since fallen away. At the Palazzo Rucellai, Alberti has taken this structural element and rendered it as pure decoration, imitating its form while enlarging it to a scale that divorces it still further from its original context. We thus encounter both pretence and the vaunting of that pretence – a kind of simultaneous masking and unmasking akin to Alberti's striving to convince onlookers of the effortlessness of his walking, riding and speaking, on the one hand, and his revealing of just how much effort this required, in his autobiography, on the other.

55 An example of Roman *opus reticulatum*.

If masking is at stake in these buildings, then we might ask
to what end. Is it simply for the pleasure of it? Perhaps when
he has Momus celebrate the power of dissimulation Alberti
really speaks for himself. Momus, however, is a different kind
of architect – *architectum elegantem omnis malitiae* (elegant architect of all kinds of malice), as he calls himself – a figure who
undoubtedly signals the darker potentialities of the power
inherent in architectural practice but who is not straightforwardly identifiable with Alberti, the designer of churches and
palaces.[34] What Alberti does seek to do, both in these buildings and in his writing, is to unsettle the viewer or reader, to
disturb the reality effect and thereby force us to abandon pas-
sivity and enter into dialogue with what we see.[35] The same
perhaps applies to the mixing of temporalities and models,
something that is also on display at the Palazzo Rucellai – not
in the same way as at the Tempio, since the facade does not

56 The Colosseum, Rome, 70–80 CE.

have to contend with any visible pre-existing fabric, but in the meeting of an edifice that recalls the contemporary Palazzo Medici with the storied orders of ancient buildings such as the Colosseum (illus. 56).[36] This compacting of temporal strata seems to have been pursued not so much with a view to denying time, but, on the contrary, in order to explore the possibilities inherent in architecture to compress, fold and concentrate history.[37] The procedure is somewhat analogous to the approach in *Momus*, where the work is set in a strangely flattened antiquity comprising different periods of the ancient world.

THE RUCELLAI BULDINGS

The Palazzo Rucellai belongs to a suite of buildings – including a loggia (illus. 57), located in the piazza in front of the palace, a funerary monument consisting of a small 'copy' of the Holy Sepulchre (illus. 58), and the facade of the church of Santa Maria Novella (illus. 59) – that were all constructed under the patronage of Giovanni Rucellai. As we have seen, no document links Alberti to the Rucellai Palace in the fifteenth century. However, the idea that he was the designer is not a modern invention. The tradition in fact dates to the sixteenth century, when a number of writers name Alberti as the architect of not only the palace but the loggia, the church facade and the Holy Sepulchre monument, suggesting that he was in command of a substantial architectural campaign.[38] Ultimately, however, all of these attributions appear to derive from a single source: not the patrician Giovanni Rucellai but the writer Giorgio Vasari. In the *Vite*, Vasari named Alberti as the sole designer of all of these structures, although, when he spoke of the palace, he called the patron Cosimo rather than Giovanni. However, Vasari's account is not entirely clear cut, since in the 1550 edition, he attributed only the doorway of the church to Alberti, while in the 1568 version he gave him the whole facade. In both cases, he specified that Alberti provided the *disegno*, which might suggest a drawing specifically.[39] This accords with the statement that Fra Giovanni di Carlo (or Caroli) allegedly made in the fifteenth century as part of a collection of lives of notable brothers of Santa Maria Novella, dedicated to Cristoforo Landino. There, he is supposed to have said that the 'celebrated architect' Leon Battista Alberti had designed the marble inlay of the church's facade. Both di Carlo's position as a Dominican at the convent of Santa

57 Rucellai Loggia, Florence.

Maria Novella and his proximity to Landino, who was himself a close friend of Alberti, would have put him in a good
position to know. However, Mancini, who reports di Carlo's
words, had not seen the manuscript himself, and instead
relied on an eighteenth-century biography of Alberti by
Pompilio Pozzetti. In fact, it seems certain that Caroli never
wrote any such thing.[40] Meanwhile, another member of the

58 Rucellai Sepulchre, San Pancrazio, Florence.

convent in the fifteenth century, Fra Domenico di Giovanni da Corella, also commented on the facade, naming only the mason Giovanni di Bertino as its maker and omitting any mention of Alberti.

The evidence, then, is fragile and indecisive.[41] There is little documentation for projects such as the Santa Maria Novella facade, and even if there were more, we might not

59 Santa Maria Novella, Florence. The facade was completed in 1470.

expect Alberti's name to appear, since as a non-professional his involvement might have been more informal in nature. The situation is such that those who are opposed to the idea that Alberti could have designed significant buildings – those who recoil at the very notion of a writer being capable of such practical undertakings – will find the evidence flimsy enough to dismiss out of hand. Contrarily, those wedded to an encomiastic view of Alberti as a great Renaissance master-architect will believe their positions to be fully supported. The first group will consider themselves confronted by a myth, the second group by history.

Vasari, who was later involved in the interior remodelling of Santa Maria Novella, cannot simply be dismissed. However, since his attribution was made almost a century after the buildings were erected, it cannot be considered to be reliable. This makes Alberti's authorship of Rucellai's architectural works tenuous at best. Even if Vasari is right, and Alberti was in some sense 'the architect', then he must have worked in collaboration with Bertino as his executor, just as he did with others on all of his documented projects, and we can assume that the Florentine mason would have played a significant role.[42] Regardless of what Alberti might say in *De re aedificatoria*, his correspondence with Matteo de' Pasti shows him to be far from an all-controlling, jealous guardian of his schemes. He defends his views against those of competitors, dismissing the opinions of a certain 'Manetto' regarding the proposed dome, and, as we have seen, insisting on maintaining funda-mental proportional relationships. But he also urges Matteo to consult widely: 'listen to many and let me know', since 'someone might say something worthwhile.' No doubt Matteo himself had much to say and he probably contributed substantially to the project. If both Alberti and Bertino were involved with the facade of Santa Maria Novella, a similar situation might have held sway.

THE SANTA MARIA NOVELLA FACADE

At Santa Maria Novella, matters are especially complicated. Once again, the project involved alterations to a pre-existing building, this time a very large Dominican church dating from the thirteenth and fourteenth centuries, facing onto a spacious piazza. The lower part of the facade was encrusted with marble inlay, but quite how far up the building this extended is not clear. At this lower level, there stood a series of *avelli*, or openings for tombs, contained within broad gothic arches. The project of completion had to contend with these elements. At the Tempio Malatestiano, Alberti had encased the old church in a new outer layer. Here, the facade would instead extend what was already there, sympathetically continuing its chromatic order while introducing a markedly *all'antica* system of ornament. The result is an intensely patterned, geometrical, polychrome facade of extraordinary subtlety. Indeed, for some, it is simply too good to be the work of an amateur and must depend entirely on a master mason trained in the Florentine tradition – presumably Bertino. And yet it is not beyond credibility that Alberti, skilled in geometry, deeply engaged in architectural design, resident for long periods in Florence and profoundly attached to the conspicuously marbled church of San Miniato, could have created something of this kind.

At the lowest level of the facade, the gothic arches, as we have seen, were already in place. Quite probably some of the marble panelling above them was there too, and it is possible that the slender pilasters, and the arches above them, also existed. What was certainly added to the lowest storey were the four engaged columns, the two pillars at either end, and the pilasters and the central portal, an exquisite creation that strongly reflects the influence of the Pantheon. All of this was capped off with a full, ancient-style entablature: the stone-work band, made up of what are known as the architrave, frieze and cornice, which in Greco-Roman architecture traditionally runs above and is supported (actually or notionally) by columns or pilasters. Here, the entablature projects forwards over the columns and the piers, in a fashion that is reminiscent of both the Tempio Malatestiano and other Roman triumphal arches that Alberti would have known, such as the Arch of Constantine. Above the entablature rises a mezzanine or attic level containing further geometrical patterning, book-ended by forms that seem to extend the piers below and capped off with a cornice. This in turn supports the top part, which incorporates the pre-existing round window and is divided by pilasters into three bays, the middle of which is twice as wide as the two that flank it. A further entablature and pediment crown the whole ensemble. Effectively, the orders are used here to create a system that projects in front of the pre-existing facade and imposes control upon it.[43]

In architectural history survey courses, the facade will often be pointed to as an early solution to a problem facing Renaissance architects wanting to build in an *all'antica* style. The majority of churches were modelled on basilicas, long buildings with a wide, central aisle, and often with narrower side aisles, rising to a lower level, on either side. Developed in ancient times as courts of law, the remains of prominent examples of basilicas still stand close to the forum area in Rome. However, humanists such as Alberti referred to churches as temples, and had good reason to believe that, as part of the recovery of ancient architecture, churches should be given facades resembling temple fronts: porches in which columns support a pedimented roof. The difficulty was that such temple fronts do not fit happily onto basilicas, not least because the side aisles get in the way. Santa Maria Novella presents one solution to this problem. The lower level and the mezzanine run right across the central aisle (normally referred to in a church as the 'nave') and the side aisles, and in fact extend a little beyond them. The top level covers the clerestory, the part of the nave that rises up high above the level of the side aisles. This area can then be treated as though it were indeed the front of a temple, with columns – or, as here, pilasters – supporting a pediment. The use of the mezzanine is important as a means to project a classical-seeming proportional scheme onto the unruly dimensions of the basilica. While imitating the attic storey of a triumphal arch, it also covers part of the roofs of the aisles, and ensures that the columns are not so high that they would have to be exceptionally wide, and that on the upper level the pilasters need not be elongated and either widened or narrowed out of all proportion with the pediment above them. Nonetheless, the transition from mezzanine to clerestory level would be abrupt, were it not for the addition of the two scroll-like volutes on either side, which help to conceal the aisle roofs and which provide a smooth

60 Baptistery of San Giovanni, Florence; exterior marble inlay completed in the 13th century.

linkage between the different parts of the building. Alberti was concerned with this problem at the Tempio Malatestiano also, and in his letter to Matteo de' Pasti he provided a drawing of the shape that he wanted to use in that instance, although the design was not executed.

The temple front thus found its place at Santa Maria Novella, though very much in the form of a representation. There is no deep porch but something more like a flattened-out image that refers back to a previous building type, an effect that is enhanced by the highly pictorial character of the patterning present on every part of the surface. Once again, ancient Roman architecture is made to confront local tradition. The marble inlay recalls both the Florentine Baptistery

61 San Miniato, Florence. The facade was begun in the 11th century.

(illus. 60) and the church of San Miniato (illus. 61), the latter of which features prominently in two Albertian dialogues, *De iciarchia* and *Profugiorum*, and seems to have been the object of special reverence by Alberti. At Santa Maria Novella, the parallels with San Miniato are so striking as to be immediately apparent from even the most cursory comparison of the buildings. The engaged columns made from green 'verde di Prato' marble and the clerestory level divided into three bays by four pilasters are common to both of them. The blind arcade of the medieval church finds its echo in the arches of the marble patterning at Santa Maria Novella (a detail that might pre-date the Renaissance project) and the earlier building is also capped off with a feature that recalls a pediment. Like Santa Maria Novella, San Miniato includes transitional forms, in the shape of simple, triangular wedges linking the upper and lower parts of the facade. And just as at Santa Maria Novella, the makers of the Romanesque facade also seem to have meditated deeply upon the meeting of temple and basilica, producing a solution that, in its imagistic flattening and layering, would have appealed greatly to Alberti. Perhaps the strongest link between the two of them is simply that Santa Maria Novella's polychrome marble facade is the first to have been constructed for any church in Florence since the time of San Miniato.[44]

In some ways, the Santa Maria Novella facade might seem to speak to the entire range of Alberti's hermeneutic interests, uniting architecture, pictorial practice and text in a single artefact. Even if we accept Alberti as the overall architect, much of the fine pictorial detail must no doubt be credited to Giovanni Bertino, the master of marble intarsia. The complex geometry of the entire scheme, however, with its increasing preponderance of white marble as it rises upwards, could certainly be an Albertian invention, and it has been suggested that the elegant, classical script crediting the building of the facade to Giovanni, the son of Paolo Rucellai, in the year 1470 is also of Alberti's devising (illus. 62).[45] This bold proclamation of the patron's name stands in stark contrast to the paucity of records regarding the architects. Further references to Rucellai appear on the frieze of the entablature, where the image of a sail is repeated across its entire length. The same symbol, alluding to fortune, and the need to adapt to its caprices, can be found on the facade of Giovanni's palace. There, it is one of many different signifiers, which include the patron's coat of arms, other heraldic devices, the architectural orders, and even the more than fifty makers' marks inscribed

62 Santa Maria Novella, detail of facade.

on individual blocks of stone, that make the whole into one great shimmering semantic field; a complex grid (or mosaic) in which what we might call 'architectural Latin' is made to collide with various vernaculars in a way that would surely have pleased Alberti.[46]

MANTUA

Nautical metaphors, such as the inflated sail, were common among humanist writers, and Alberti employed them frequently.[47] Thus, while the emblem of the sail is Rucellai's own, it would also have been profoundly meaningful for Alberti, a writer who was constantly preoccupied by *fortuna*. Fortune certainly intervened in his architectural career. In 1460 he was given the chance to design an entire building from scratch: the church of San Sebastiano in Mantua. Conditions were, in many ways, optimal. The project was backed by Ludovico Gonzaga, the ruler of Mantua, a powerful patron with the will and the money to see it succeed. Having accrued experience elsewhere, Alberti now had a store of knowledge that he could apply to the design. For its execution, he could rely on a seasoned practitioner, Luca Fancelli, Ludovico's court architect. The stage, we might think, was set for the creation of a clear and lasting architectural statement. Visit the building today, however, and that is not what you will find. Instead, it is a tormented structure that has undergone successive periods of deterioration and refashioning and that now provides an imperfect sense of Alberti's original scheme (illus. 63). This is not due merely to the ravages of time. From the outset, the building was afflicted by problems that seem to have

necessitated substantial modifications. Important parts of the design were never executed, and less than thirty years after construction started the church was considered to be on the point of ruin. How did it all go so wrong?

The building history of San Sebastiano is complex and unsatisfying, and there is no way of piecing it together without making some big speculative leaps. Here, we can allow ourselves only the most bare-boned summary.[48] Alberti's relations with Mantua's ruling family were longstanding. Connections were reinforced when in 1459 he travelled to Mantua in the train of Pope Pius II for a council held to drum up support for a campaign against the Turks. Shortly afterwards, he was in correspondence with Ludovico Gonzaga regarding a number of architectural projects, among which San Sebastiano was quickly given priority. It was to be located on the periphery of the city, close to its southern gate, a site that might already have housed a shrine to the saint, though there is no sign of any

63 San Sebastiano, Mantua, begun 1460.

pre-existing structure. What the area certainly did have was water. Mantua was in this period almost an island, surrounded by rivers and lakes, and the land to the south was markedly damp. As a result, Ludovico ordered a huge drainage operation to prepare the ground. Following this, building proceeded apace. Quite how apace depends on how one interprets the documents, but it may be that within two years the building had already risen to the height of the chapels.[49] Documents of 1462 and 1463, however, speak of water damage to vaults and to the lower parts of the walls, suggesting that the drainage operation had not been fully effective. Alberti recommended that the vaults be covered with mats and tiles immediately, and he sent a revised plan to Ludovico. Exactly what this entailed is difficult to know (and even Ludovico Gonzaga and Luca Fancelli were left uncertain how to go ahead) but it may be that Alberti recommended raising the floor level. This would have created a space beneath the church that would allow moisture to dissipate (the level now referred to either as the crypt or the undercroft, which some argue was not an original feature of the design).

Raising the floor would of course probably result in a change of measurements and proportions and there is some evidence that this did occur. A sixteenth-century drawing by an architect called Antonio Labacco includes a plan of the building, an abbreviated sketch of the exterior and a number of measurements (illus. 64). In a strong assertion of authorship, Labacco has written, in the centre of the plan, 'di mano di messere batista alberti' (from the hand of *messere* Battista Alberti). Since his measurements do not correspond to the building itself (which he may never have seen), it is probable

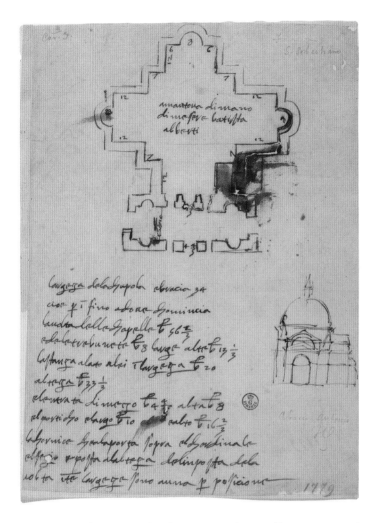

64 Antonio Labacco, plan and elevation of San Sebastiano, 16th century,
pen and ink on paper.

that he is referring to the design – perhaps Alberti's original
drawing, as the phrase 'from the hand' might imply.[50] In that
case, Labacco's acount would be the best indication of Alberti's
original scheme: a centrally planned, Greek cross church,
crowned with a large dome above and a substantial porch at

the entrance. The mismatch between the measurements he gives and those of the building could be explained by the raising of the floor level – something that itself necessitated changes to the facade, which in its final execution seems quite far from Alberti's scheme. Whatever the truth of this, work on Alberti's modified design proceeded slowly, and there was still much left to do when Alberti died in 1472. When Fancelli left the project in 1479, the year after Ludovico's death, the dome had not been built. In fact, the building lacked a proper covering until 1488, when, prompted by the poor condition of the fabric, a large groin vault was finally erected, and presumably also the pyramidal roof above.

The building that stands today in Mantua is thus a poor representation of Alberti's design: many of the original proportional relationships may have been lost; the facade has undergone drastic alterations; and the covering is of a completely different kind. We do not even know how the building was to be accessed (the current stairways are modern). What can be reasonably conjectured is that Alberti did intend a Greek cross plan with a dome above. In this sense, San Sebastiano would seem to be an early example of the Renaissance preoccupation with the construction of centrally planned churches, buildings that, unlike traditional basilicas, did not follow rectangular plans but instead adopted squares, circles and octagons, allowing the entire design to rotate around a central point. The attraction of such schemes is easy to discern. They allowed for a high degree of geometrical unity and purity, as well as proportional lucidity, and they more closely evoked some Roman temples (above all, the great, domed Pantheon in Rome), as well as the many centrally planned early Christian structures that could be seen in cities throughout Italy. When discussing the plans of temples in *De re aedificatoria*, Alberti notes that nature delights especially in the circle.[51] The clergy, however, could be resistant to such layouts, since they were deeply involved with liturgical practices that had developed from centuries of worship in basilicas with long axes. Lay people also sometimes struggled to reconcile such schemes with churches as they knew them. As a result, and notwithstanding individual chapels, many fewer centrally planned churches were built than projected in fifteenth-century Italy. San Sebastiano is among the first.

The novelty of the plan, and perhaps the entire design, certainly gave rise to comment. Ludovico's son, Cardinal Francesco Gonzaga, wrote to his father in 1474 concerning the indulgences that should be attached to the church, pointedly remarking that since it was not yet finished, the matter could not be decided. He also observed that the church was made 'in the ancient manner, similar to the fantastic vision of Messer Battista Alberti' and that for his part 'I could not tell whether he meant for it to be a church, a mosque, or a synagogue.' This seems like a form of deprecation (and in fact it has been suggested that, unlike Ludovico, neither Francesco nor his mother much cared for Alberti), but it also points to the unstable resonances of such a building.[52] Perhaps Francesco was thinking of descriptions or representations of the Dome of the Rock in Jerusalem, an Islamic building that was often, because of the site on which it stands, simply referred to as the Temple of the Lord or even the Temple of Solomon in the written accounts of European travellers. Images of the Dome, or of fantastical buildings that were loosely based on it, sometimes stood for the temple in visual art. It had briefly been made into a site of Christian worship during the crusader kingdom and it did thus constitute a good example of a famous centrally planned (octagonal), domed building that had an uncertain Muslim/Jewish/Christian identity.

Comparable structures in Italy also invited confusion regarding their origins, with the octagonal, domed Baptistery in Florence, begun in the eleventh century, sometimes believed to be an ancient Roman edifice – a converted pagan temple originally dedicated to Mars. The centrally planned building, then, by breaking from the basilical tradition, was a potentially disturbing element that might be associated with the exotic and with non-Christian religious practices (Giovanni Rucellai, for example, noted that the Early Christian church of Santo Stefano Rotondo in Rome was round and labelled it a 'temple of idols').[53] Such instability and untimeliness no doubt appealed to Alberti, and had San Sebastiano been completed as planned it would have been a powerful architectural statement. As it is, it seems at least as much like a statement about another favourite Albertian theme, fragmentation and the fragility of the whole. In *De re aedificatoria*, he is much preoccupied with the entropic forces that will assail any building, seeming to regard them as an extension of fortune's workings and urging constant vigilance. One can only imagine that he would have been dismayed but not entirely surprised by the final state of San Sebastiano. *Fortuna*, as he knew, will have her way.

SANT'ANDREA

The complications at San Sebastiano do not seem to have damaged Alberti's standing, either in Mantua or elsewhere. Indeed, from 1470, and perhaps before, he was involved in the redesign of the tribune of the important church of Santissima Annunziata in Florence, another project for which Ludovico Gonzaga was the patron. Continuing the work of Michelozzo and Antonio Manetti Ciaccheri, he once again adopted the central plan (this time a round one), and once again it must have provoked a good deal of comment, since the architect who would supervise construction wrote to Ludovico on 27 April 1471 that 'Messer Battista continues to say that it will be the most beautiful construction ever built, and that the others cannot understand it because they are not used to seeing such things, but that when they see it built, they will say that it is much more beautiful than a cruciform plan' (illus. 65).[54] This certainly sounds like Alberti, who often considered himself to be surrounded by detractors who were too envious or too ignorant to give him the credit he was due, and who clearly had not been deterred by the setbacks at San Sebastiano from believing that he knew best.

Ludovico, meanwhile, remained a firm supporter. When, in October 1470, Alberti sent him an alternative project for the rebuilding of Sant'Andrea in Mantua – an important pilgrim site on account of its relic of the Holy Blood – Ludovico seems to have been receptive. It had long been the Mantuan ruler's desire to demolish and replace the church, but the abbot who presided over the structure was implacably opposed. When the abbot died in March 1470, the way was cleared

and Ludovico could proceed. It was at this point that Alberti intervened.[55] A letter from him mentions that he was continuing to work with Luca Fancelli on inscriptions for a tower, but adds, 'I have also learned . . . that Your Lordship and your citizens have been discussing building here at Sant'Andrea, and that the chief aim was to have a large space where many people could see the Blood of Christ.' A scheme for this existed, but Alberti suggests that Ludovico consider an alternative:

> I saw Manetti's design and I liked it, but to me it does not seem suitable to your purpose. I thought and conceived of this, which I send you. It will be more capacious, more eternal, more worthy, more cheerful. It will cost much less. This type of temple was called an Etruscan shrine by the ancients. If you like it I will see to drawing it out in proportion.[56]

65 Santissima Annunziata, Florence, with the centrally planned tribune.

Ludovico responded to this with a certain cautious interest, saying: 'We have . . . seen the design which you have sent us of that temple, which in principle pleases us; but as we cannot properly understand it for ourselves, we shall wait until you are in Mantua, and then when we have spoken with you and explained our idea and understood yours, we will do what seems best.'[57] This repeats a refrain found several times in correspondence relating to Alberti's architectural works, in which patrons and site managers declare themselves unsure of his exact intentions and say that he will have to visit, or that they will send someone to visit him. The issue arises again and again in correspondence between Alberti and Ludovico, suggesting that Alberti's practice of directing works from a distance was every bit as problematic as one might imagine, and that letters and drawings often proved insufficient for making decisions on the ground. Nonetheless, it seems that Alberti did persuade Ludovico, whether in person or by letter, and in 1471 he returned to Mantua, presumably to discuss the project further. By the start of 1472 important calculations regarding materials and finance had been made. Construction would commence later that year, but not until two months after Alberti's death. It is thus to be assumed that Sant'Andrea was built, at least in some sense, according to his design, but quite what this means is not so clear. It has been suggested, based on the quantity of materials known to have been procured, that Alberti only provided a worked-out scheme for the nave of the church, leaving the crossing, transept and chancel for a later campaign; indeed, the northern end of the building was completed long afterwards, in the eighteenth century.[58]

It is generally assumed that his design included the facade, although how much detail it would have provided cannot be known (illus. 66). Certainly, the entrance portico, which projects well forward of the entry doors, almost like a building in its own right, is an extraordinary creation. Including a

66 Sant'Andrea, Mantua; design started in 1470.

sequence of coffered barrel vaults, it engenders a remarkable play of volumes and masses that is quite different from the facade of either the Tempio Malatestiano or Santa Maria Novella (illus. 67). It also involves a good deal of richly worked ornamentation, from the coffers, to the decorations on friezes, to the capitals themselves, but how much of this can be ascribed to Alberti (who produced a drawing for a capital at the Tempio Malatestiano that Matteo de' Pasti described as 'bellissima') is unknown. Four giant-order pilasters divide the facade into three bays – wider in the centre and narrower on the sides – in an arrangement reminiscent of a triumphal or honorific arch, similar to forms that Alberti had referred to elsewhere in his architecture. At the top, a large pediment covers the entire width, as at San Sebastiano. Presumably all of this was finished by 1488, since in that year the artist Andrea Mantegna painted a fresco in the roundel.[59]

The enormous entrance arch is deeply arresting, producing an effect similar to the great *pishtaq* gates found in some

67 Sant'Andrea, interior of the porch.

Islamic buildings (a famous example being the Taj Mahal). There is also now a sophisticated game of being and representation played with the architectural orders. That is to say, the smaller pilasters that stand on either side of the central arch, supporting the lower entablature, are made entirely from finely carved stone. However, the shafts of the giant-order pilasters (pilasters that run up the full height of the facade, passing straight through the lower entablature) are not markedly distinguished from the rest of the wall surface, albeit they were probably once painted. The stucco frames that define them seem more like the borders of shallow, empty boxes. Originally, the capitals above them were also of stucco, while the bases were apparently made from terra cotta.[60] The effect draws attention to the purely decorative nature of these giant orders, whose shafts appear almost as drawings rather than solid objects. Their obliteration of the lower entablature, which seems to disappear behind them, further undermines any sense that the orders of the facade are part of a structural system.

In a perceptive essay, the architectural historian Rudolf Wittkower characterized Alberti as achieving here a particularly effective unity of orders and wall. These elements, he proposed, stood in an ambiguous tension in Alberti's architectural theory, with columns being regarded sometimes as ornaments and at other times as sections of wall; a problem that Wittkower argued Alberti engaged with throughout his architectural works.[61] Here, the distinction appears almost to have been abolished. Prior to an overzealous twentieth-century restoration, it seems that the facade displayed a good deal of painted ornamentation, something that might also be true of San Sebastiano. This suggests that Alberti (or Ludovico or Luca Fancelli) was not prepared to forego coloured patterning even when the budget did not allow for stone incrustation.[62] The result must have been a peculiar combination of the tectonic and the imagistic. Combined with its seemingly too-large central opening and tightly stacked lateral bays, the facade is strange and original, contriving to feel at once naive, refined, and knowingly artificial, while also in parts radiating a rich and profound *romanitas* (Roman-ness).

As we have seen, however, Alberti described his design to Ludovico not as Roman but as Etruscan. In his architectural treatise, he discusses the design of Etruscan temples in a difficult passage that has been the subject of much interpretation.[63]

68 Sant'Andrea, interior.

Undoubtedly, he had a particular reverence for the Etruscan civilization, which he saw as a truly 'Italic' form of antiquity, and which he credited with an especially important role in bringing architecture to perfection. Momus, when he falls through the sky, lands not in Attica or even in Rome but in Etruria, which Alberti treats as a kind of all-encompassing antique world. For Ludovico, an Etruscan-style temple might have carried with it the frisson of both the exotic and the indigenous. In proposing it, Alberti vaunted a particular form of architectural expertise, derived in part from a deep archaeological and philological understanding of ancient history. The church interior certainly presents a magnificent space: a great, wide nave, presumably made to accommodate crowds of pilgrims and allow them a good view of the relic, is topped with a long barrel vault (illus. 68). There are no aisles. Instead, barrel-vaulted chapels are separated by enormous piers. On the faces of those piers, giant-order pilasters flank round windows, which let in a diffused light and echo the windows of the chapels and the facade. Despite Alberti's Etruscan claims, the building has the feel of imperial Roman architecture, conceived in terms of volumes and masses. It aspires to a form of grandeur that does not really have a precedent in fifteenth-century building but that would become a preoccupation of architects thereafter.

Even from a very brief and selective survey such as this one, the problems of writing about Alberti's architecture become apparent. That he *can* be called an architect seems to me self-evident, provided that one does not apply an excessively restrictive definition of what an architect is. Alberti had a writer's training and spent the greater part of his life pursuing a literary career. However, there is no lack of evidence to show that he designed buildings and was considered an expert, both by local, 'executive' architects who collaborated with him, and by patrons who had the money and the power to make his projects happen. One need only consider how Ludovico Gonzaga writes to him, acknowledging 'the great authority that you have with everyone, and especially with us, such that we would not consider going either forwards or backwards with the works without your say so'.[64]

To gain a true picture of Alberti *as* an architect is, however, a difficult task. The Tempio Malatestiano is incomplete. The buildings for Giovanni Rucellai were not attributed to him until later. No documents generated from the projects themselves at the moment of construction confirm Alberti's participation. Even Vasari's account of Santa Maria Novella indicates a hesitation, with the attribution to Alberti first of the portal and then of the whole facade. At San Sebastiano, we can be sure of Alberti's involvement, but significant aspects of the design are lost. The best evidence for its reconstruction rests on the interpretation of a sixteenth-century drawing that seems likely (but is not certain) to follow Alberti's original, made by a man who had probably never seen the building itself. At Sant'Andrea, we know that Alberti provided a design and that he visited Mantua shortly afterwards. Yet we also know that even the best laid plans are likely to undergo change, and the fact is that Alberti was dead before construction had even started. We are thus compelled to contemplate the elusive quality of history with which the humanists were so often confronted. Looking over this assortment of buildings we may be struck by their playful and erudite eclecticism, their frequent recourse to local models as well as prominent ancient buildings in Rome, and the manner in which they exploit the tension between seeming and being, image and structure, and old and new. Here and there we catch glimpses (real or imagined) of Alberti, who seems to move through the scene like a winged eye: sometimes a dynamic, motivating force, at other times an intangible abstraction. So: *quid tum?*

Epilogue

attista Alberti made his will on 19 April 1472 as he lay ill at his home in Rome. By 25 April he was dead. He chose as his universal heir his cousin Bernardo, who would receive all of his share of the palace of Benedetto di Nerozzo and the main Bolognese properties.[1] Battista also set aside money for the purchase of a house in Bologna for the use of up to two students from the Alberti family. Supported by income from other properties, those living there could read canon or civil law, or any other discipline at the university. Any young Alberti could apply, and while the male line was always to be given priority, females were also eligible. This rather gives the lie to Alberti's statements regarding the intellectual limitations of women, just as the arrangement as a whole suggests that his negative remarks about his law degree in Bologna were not the entire story. Should there be no Alberti applicants to this fund, then support ought instead to be given to two poor students from outside of the family, to be selected by the executors of the will. With these provisions, Alberti presumably hoped to help any future Philoponius who might arise. He also sought as much as possible to sustain the family. The will stipulated that after Bernardo's death, the property granted to him would pass to his heirs. If Bernardo's line came to an end, it would go to the next closest Alberti relatives. Only in the event that the entire *consorteria* was extinguished would it pass to the hospital of Santa Maria Nuova, and even then it could never be sold, only rented out for up to three years at a time.

Alberti stipulated that his funeral was to take place in the church of Sant'Agostino in Rome, where he would temporarily be laid to rest. However, his body should then in due course be transported to Padua and interred in his father's tomb in the Basilica del Santo.[2] Thus, at the very end of his life, Alberti still yearned to be close to Lorenzo, the father whose will had brought his illegitimate son so much strife. It is also notable that, however strong his feelings might have been regarding his initial arrival in Florence, and however attached he might have become to Rome, it was to Padua – the city of his childhood, the place where Barzizza had taught him to be a humanist and the resting place of his father – that he wanted ultimately to return. But it was not to be. Two of the executors gave their authority to the third, Antonio Grassi, a jurist and archpriest of the Cathedral of Bologna, to manage Alberti's estate. After an initial period in which no suitable applicants for the scholarship could be found, Grassi abandoned the scheme and instead opened a fund to support choirboys; it was not called Collegio degli Alberti but Collegio Grassi.[3] Alberti's body was never brought to Padua. Having been entombed in Sant'Agostino, he remained there until, just a few years later, the church was substantially rebuilt. The tombs were cleared and his burial site was lost.

Examining the wills of both Lorenzo and Battista, it is striking how both failed to control large parts of their legacy.

Not only did Battista not receive what Lorenzo had left to him, but he ended up possessing those things that his father had insisted he never should have. Battista could not effect his post-mortem reconciliation with his father or his support for the young scholars of his *consorteria*. Despite all of the stern injunctions of the wills, framed in the legal language of absolute prohibitions and enduring prescriptions, neither Lorenzo, with his immense wealth, nor Battista, with his extraordinary intelligence, could make some of their most basic desires into realities. *Fortuna*, it seems, found no difficulty in undoing the schemes of plutocrats and intellectuals. Even great potentates often failed to get their way. Sigismondo Malatesta, for example, strenuously desired that his son Roberto should complete the Tempio Malatestiano. Roberto, however, showed little interest in the project, though he did perfect the building in miniature form, having his chefs sculpt both the Tempio and the Castel Sismondo in sugar to decorate his wedding banquet.[4]

We have seen that Alberti was intensely concerned with the question of will, whether it be in painting or in household management, and with the knowledge and techniques that could make will sovereign by uniting it with power. However, he was also conscious of the limits of all such techniques – conscious of their ultimate failure, of the breakdown of every ideal order, and of the inevitable dissolution and fragmentation of things. Even painting, which seemed to hold out the promise of a perfect fusion of mathematical reasoning and moral wisdom, was really only an attempt to 'embrace the surface', born from the impossible desire of 'that Narcissus who was converted into a flower'.

Flowers feature prominently in several of Alberti's works, and they are also visible in the last known portrait of him: an anonymous drawing that some believe to be a self-portrait. Sketched into a manuscript of the *Profugiorum*, it depicts him pointing to his name, and maybe also his own text, with an elongated finger (see illus. 1).[5] Here, the flowers may indicate that Alberti should be conceived of as standing at one of his favourite vantage points – somewhere on the 'outside', surrounded by nature, looking in. Simultaneously, the flowers might allude to his poetic and painterly qualities, while also pointing to the strange position of the author, whose brief life will (like the beauty of flowers) pass even as his works persist. A line in the opening part of Alberti's testament, which seems altogether too poetic to belong to the legal official and has therefore been considered by some to constitute Battista Alberti's final literary work, addresses precisely such sentiments. In fact, since it paraphrases the book of Job (14:2), perhaps by way of St Augustine, it might even be thought of as the last tessera in Alberti's literary mosaic. Touching upon the themes of dissolution and impermanence that haunt so many of his writings, it reads: 'man, like a flower, vanishes and dissolves and flees like a shadow, and never continues in the same state.'[6]

CHRONOLOGY

1437	Collapse of the Alberti banking businesses. Alberti produces the second version of *Philodoxeos*, revealing his authorship
1438	Alberti probably follows the curia to Ferrara. The *Vita* is composed around this time
1440	A notarial document places Alberti in Florence. The *Theogenius* was probably written around this time
1441	Alberti stages *Certame coronario*, a poetry contest, at Florence cathedral
1442	*Profugiorum ab erumna libri III* perhaps written this year, and almost certainly before 1444
1447	Alberti attempts to raise a sunken Roman barge from the bed of Lake Nemi
1448	Giovanni Rucellai makes improvements to his house, initiating a long campaign of building projects
1450	Around this time Alberti writes *Ex ludis rerum mathematicarum* (The Mathematical Games)
1452	Alberti presents his architectural treatise, *De re aedificatoria*, to Pope Nicholas V
1454	Letter to Matteo de' Pasti on the Tempio Malatestiano
1459	Alberti travels to Mantua with Pope Pius II
1460	Sigismondo Malatesta excommunicated and condemned as a citizen of hell. Work begins on the facade of Santa Maria Novella in Florence. Alberti begins the project for San Sebastiano in Mantua
1461	Sigismondo Malatesta falls from power and work on the church of San Francesco ceases. Work begins on the Rucellai Sepulchre at San Pancrazio, Florence
1462	First indications of water damage at San Sebastiano
1463	Alberti is present in Mantua in connection with the construction of San Sebastiano
1468	Alberti is awarded a large share of the palace built by his grandfather, Benedetto di Nerozzo, in Florence as well as several properties in Bologna
1470	Alberti writes to Ludovico Gonzaga regarding Sant'Andrea in Mantua
1471	Alberti visits Mantua

1472	Alberti dies in Rome
1479	Initiation of works on the nave of Sant'Agostino in Rome, probably leading to the destruction of Alberti's tomb
1485	First printed edition of *De re aedificatoria*
1488	Groin vault erected over San Sebastiano, finally covering the building

REFERENCES

Introduction

1 See Julius von Schlosser, *Ein Künstlerproblem der Renaissance: Leon Battista Alberti* (Vienna and Leipzig, 1929); translated into Italian by Giovanna Federici Ajroldi as 'Problemi artistici nella prima Rinascenza italiana, I: Il non artista: Leon Battista Alberti', in von Schlosser, *Xenia: Saggi sulla storia dello stile e del linguaggio nell'arte figurative* (Bari, 1938), pp. 9–46.

1 Exile and Return

1 Owing to its greater fluidity, I have used Cecil Grayson's translation throughout, with some minor alterations and additions. See Leon Battista Alberti, *On Painting and On Sculpture: The Latin Texts of De pictura and De statua*, ed. and trans. Cecil Grayson (London, 1972), p. 33. Also indispensable are Rocco Sinisgalli, *Il nuovo 'De pictura' di Leon Battista Alberti = The New 'De pictura' of Leon Battista Alberti* (Rome, 2006), which contains a new translation and compares previous translations of the text; and the new critical edition in Leon Battista Alberti, *De pictura (redazione volgare)*, ed. Lucia Bertolini (Florence, 2011).
2 Alberti, *On Painting*, p. 33.
3 On this idea see Christine Smith, *Architecture in the Culture of Early Humanism: Ethics, Aesthetics and Eloquence, 1400–1470* (New York, 1992), pp. 19–53.
4 Luigi Passerini, *Gli Alberti di Firenze: genealogia, storia, e documenti* (Florence, 1869), vol. II, pp. 351–86.

5 For a concise summary of the system of government see Gene
   Brucker, *Renaissance Florence*, 2nd edn (Berkeley, CA, 1983),
   pp. 128–37; for an account of Florence's 21 guilds, see John
   M. Najemy, *A History of Florence, 1200–1575* (Malden, MA, 2006),
   pp. 39–44.

6 Passerini, *Gli Alberti di Firenze*, vol. I, p. 7.

7 Susannah Kerr Foster, 'The Ties That Bind: Kinship Association
   and Marriage in the Alberti Family, 1378–1428', PhD thesis,
   Cornell University, 1985, p. 3; and Passerini, *Gli Alberti di Firenze*, vol.
   I, pp. xi–xii, 9–11.

8 Foster, 'The Ties That Bind', pp. 5–6.

9 The classic account of the fall of the Bardi and Peruzzi banks is in
   Armando Sapori, *La crisi delle compagnie mercantile dei Bardi e dei Peruzzi*
   (Florence, 1926); for an analysis that revises the role traditionally
   ascribed to the English monarchy, see Edwin S. Hunt, 'A New
   Look at the Dealings of the Bardi and Peruzzi with Edward III',
   Journal of Economic History, L/I (1990), pp. 149–62.

10 Foster, 'The Ties That Bind', p. 6; for an account of the early phase
   of the Alberti businesses see Raymond de Roover, 'The Story of
   the Alberti Company of Florence, 1302–1348, as Revealed in Its
   Accounts Books', *Business History Review*, XXXII/I (1958), pp. 14–59.

11 *Istorie pistolesi, ovvero delle cose avvenute in Toscana dall'anno MCCC al
   MCCCXLVIII e Diario del Monaldi* (Milan, 1845), pp. 443–4; and
   Passerini, *Gli Alberti di Firenze*, vol. I, p. 16.

12 George Holmes, 'Florentine Merchants in England, 1346–1436',
   Economic History Review, New Series, XIII/8 (1960), pp. 193–208,
   here 193.

13 Passerini, *Gli Alberti di Firenze*, p. 13.

14 Ibid., pp. xi, 12.

15 Ibid., pp. 29–31; Foster, 'The Ties That Bind', p. 7.

16 For a concise account of the Ciompi revolution and its aftermath
   see Najemy, *A History of Florence*, pp. 161–71.

17 Ibid., p. 186.

18 Ibid.

19 Passerini, *Gli Alberti di Firenze*, vol. I, pp. 124–5.

20 Ibid., vol. I, pp. 32–3, 125–6, 162–3; for the relevant documents,
   vol. II, pp. 231–40.

21 For a summary of these measures see Susannah Foster Baxendale, 'Exile in Practice: The Alberti Family In and Out of Florence, 1401–1428', *Renaissance Quarterly*, XLIV/4 (1991), pp. 720–56, especially pp. 725–30.

22 Foster Baxendale, 'Exile in Practice', explores the history of the Alberti exile in detail and demonstrates the important role played by Alberti women.

23 Ibid., pp. 737–9.

24 Passerini, *Gli Alberti di Firenze*, vol. II, pp. 47–9.

25 Leonardo Bruni, trans., *Panegyric to the City of Florence*, in *The Earthly Republic: Italian Humanists on Government and Society*, ed. B. G. Kohl, R. Witt and E. Welles (Philadelphia, PA, 1978), pp. 135–75, here 144–5. I have slightly modified the translation.

26 Randolph Starn, *Contrary Commonwealth: The Theme of Exile in Medieval and Renaissance Italy* (Berkeley, CA, 1982).

27 On Alberti's birth date and the horoscope, see Roberto Cardini, 'Un nuovo reperto Albertiano', *Moderni e antichi: quaderni del Centro di Studi sul Classicismo II–III* (2004–5), pp. 81–100. For the document identifying Alberti's mother, see Carlo Ceschi, 'La madre di Leon Battista Alberti', *Bolletino d'arte*, 4th series, XXXIII (1948), pp. 191–2. For the argument that it is false, see Paola Massalin, 'Una nuova fonte sulla nascita dell'Alberti: il MS. *Conv. Sopp. I.IX.3 della Biblioteca Nazionale di Firenze*', *Albertiana*, VII (2004), pp. 237–46; and Roberto Cardini, 'Biografia, leggi e astrologia in un nuovo reperto Albertiano', in *Leon Battista Alberti umanista e scrittore: filologia, esegesi, tradizione. Atti del Convegno internazionale del Comitato Nazionale VI centenario della nascita di Leon Battista Alberti, Arezzo 24–25 giugno 2004* (Florence, 2007), vol. I, pp. 21–189, especially, p. 28, n. 18. On Alberti's brother Carlo, see Alberto Martelli's biographical essay in Carlo Alberti, *Tutti gli scritti*, ed. Alberto Martelli (Florence, 2015), pp. 47–56.

28 On Battista's illegitimacy and the actions that his father could have taken, see Thomas Kuehn, 'Reading Between the Patrilines: Leon Battista Alberti's "Della Famiglia" in Light of His Illegitimacy', *I Tatti Studies in the Italian Renaissance*, 1 (1985), pp. 161–87; and 'Leon Battista Alberti come illegittimo Fiorentino', in *La vita e il mondo di Leon Battista Alberti: atti dei Convegni internazionali del Comitato nazionale*

VI *centenario della nascita di Leon Battista Alberti, Genova, 19–21 febbraio 2004* (Florence, 2008), vol. I, pp. 147–71.

29 Foster Baxendale, 'Exile in Practice', p. 746; Girolamo Mancini, *Vita di Leon Battista Alberti*, 2nd edn (Florence, 1911), p. 24.

30 On this see Laurence E. Hooper, 'Exile and Petrarch's Reinvention of Authorship', *Renaissance Quarterly*, LXIX/4 (2006), pp. 1217–56.

2 Blossoms and Scorpions

1 Leon Battista Alberti, *Opere volgari*, ed. Cecil Grayson (Bari, 1960–66), vol. II, pp. 160–61.

2 Ibid., p. 161.

3 Roberto Cardini, *Mosaici: il 'nemico' dell'Alberti* (Rome, 1990).

4 For an overview of humanism see Christopher S. Celenza, 'Humanism', in *The Classical Tradition*, ed. Anthony Grafton, Glenn W. Most and Salvatore Settis (Cambridge, MA, 2010), pp. 426–67. Nicholas Mann, 'The Origins of Humanism', in *The Cambridge Companion to Renaissance Humanism*, ed. Jill Kraye (Cambridge, 1996), pp. 1–19, discusses medieval humanism before the fifteenth century and provides a broad definition of humanism itself on p. 2. See also Martin McLaughlin, 'Leon Battista Alberti and the Redirection of Renaissance Humanism', *Proceedings of the British Academy*, CLXVII (2010), pp. 25–59, here 28.

5 Quoted in Wayne A. Rebhorn, *Renaissance Debates on Rhetoric* (Ithaca, NY, 2000), p. 20.

6 On Petrarch, see Christopher S. Celenza, *Petrarch: Everywhere a Wanderer* (London, 2017). On Alberti and Petrarch, see David Marsh, 'Petrarch and Alberti', in *Renaissance Studies in Honour of Craig Hugh Smyth*, ed. Andrew Morrogh et al. (Florence, 1985), vol. I, pp. 363–75; and McLaughlin, 'Leon Battista Alberti and the Redirection'.

7 R.G.G. Mercer, *The Teaching of Gasparino Barzizza, with Special Reference to His Place in Paduan Humanism* (London, 1979), pp. 44–5, 106–17.

8 On the study of law in Italy in this period, and the approaches taken at the two foremost centres of Padua and Bologna, see Paul F. Grendler, *The Universities of the Italian Renaissance* (Baltimore, MD, 2002), pp. 430–36, 447–56.

9   On Alberti's education and his formation in Padua and Bologna,
    see especially Peter Francis Weller, 'Alberti before Florence: Early
    Sources Informing Leon Battista Alberti's De Pictura', PhD thesis,
    UCLA, 2014, pp. 39–244.

10 A parallel translation of the play can be found in *Humanist Comedies*,
    ed. and trans. Gary R. Grund (Cambridge, MA, 2005), pp. 70–169;
    for the quotation see Anthony Grafton, *Leon Battista Alberti: Master
    Builder of the Italian Renaissance* (New York, 2000), p. 4.

11 Girolamo Mancini, *Vita di Leon Battista Alberti*, 2nd edn (Florence,
    1911), pp. 45–6.

12 On this see McLaughlin, 'Leon Battista Alberti and the
    Redirection', pp. 34–5; Lucia Bertolini, *Grecus sapor: tramiti di presenze
    greche in Leon Battista Alberti* (Rome, 1998); and Timothy Kircher,
    *Living Well in Renaissance Italy: The Virtues of Humanism and the Irony of
    Leon Battista Alberti* (Tempe, AZ, 2012), p. 213.

13 Leon Battista Alberti, *The Use and Abuse of Books: De commodis
    litterarum atque incommodis*, trans. Renée Neu Watkins
    (Prospect Heights, N\, 1999), p. 21.

14 On this see Watkins's introduction, ibid., p. 4.

15 Alberti, *The Use and Abuse of Books*, p. 41.

16 On this topic see Stefano Cracolici, 'Flirting with the Chameleon:
    Alberti on Love', *MLN*, 121 (2006), pp. 102–29.

17 In scenes 4 and 5 alone he uses the imperative 'tace' (be quiet)
    seven times.

18 Alberti, *The Use and Abuse of Books*, p. 24. I have slightly modified
    the translation.

19 On this see Cracolici, 'Flirting with the Chameleon'; and 'I
    percorsi divergenti del dialogo d'amore: la "Deifira" di L. B.
    Alberti e i suoi "doppi"', *Albertiana*, 2 (1999), pp. 137–67.

20 Cracolici, 'Flirting with the Chameleon', pp. 121–2.

21 Alberti, *Opere volgari*, vol. III, p. 245.

22 Alberti, *The Use and Abuse of Books*, p. 24.

23 See Cardini's commentary in Leon Battista Alberti, *Opere latine*
    (Rome, 2010), p. 119. The same publication, pp. 91–121, includes
    the Latin text, with an Italian translation by M. Letizia Bracciali
    Magnini and notes by Cardini, in collaboration with Mariangela
    Regoliosi.

24 On Alberti and elegy in relation to the *Deifira*, see Roberto Cardini, 'La rifondazione albertiana dell'elegia. Smontaggio della Deifira', in *Alberti e la tradizione: per lo 'smontaggio' dei 'mosaici' albertiani*, ed. R. Cardini and M. Regoliosi, 2 vols (Florence, 2007), vol. I, pp. 305–56.

25 On this see Luca Boschetto, *Leon Battista Alberti e Firenze: biografia, storia, letteratura* (Florence, 2000), p. 75; and McLaughlin, 'Leon Battista Alberti and the Redirection', pp. 46–51.

26 McLaughlin, 'Leon Battista Alberti and the Redirection'; see also Anthony Grafton, *Commerce with the Classics: Ancient Books and Renaissance Readers* (Ann Arbor, MI, 1997), pp. 53–92.

27 Martin McLaughlin, 'Alberti and the Classical Canon', in *Italy and the Classical Tradition: Language, Thought and Poetry, 1300–1600*, ed. Carlo Caruso and Andrew Laird (London, 2009), pp. 73–100.

28 Alberti, *The Use and Abuse of Books*, p. 16.

29 Kircher, *Living Well*, especially chap. I.

30 Alberti, *The Use and Abuse of Books*, p. 49.

31 Renée Neu Watkins, 'Leon Battista Alberti in the Mirror: An Interpretation of the *Vita* with a New Translation', *Italian Quarterly*, XXX/117 (1989), pp. 5–30, here 7.

3 Painting

1 The passages above are from the translation in Leon Battista Alberti, *Dinner Pieces*, trans. David Marsh (Binghamton, N\, 1987), pp. 54–7.

2 Frances Yates, *The Art of Memory* (London, 1966) is the fundamental work on the artificial memory from antiquity to the early modern period. On memory in the Middle Ages, see also Mary Carruthers, *The Book of Memory: A Study of Memory in the Medieval Culture*, 2nd edn (Cambridge, 1990). Alberti's extravagant figures in the *Paintings* might be compared to those of the late antique writer Martianus Capella, who in his *De nuptiis Philologiae et Mercurii* (On the Marriage of Philology and Mercury) described striking personifications of the liberal arts.

3 Leon Battista Alberti, *The Use and Abuse of Books: De commodis litterarum atque incommodis*, trans. Renée Neu Watkins (Prospect Heights, N\, 1999), p. 24.

4 Lucia Bertolini, 'Sulla precedenza della redazione volgare del
   De pictura di Leon Battista Alberti', in *Studi per Umberto Carpi. Un
   saluto da allievi e colleghi pisani*, ed. Marco Santagata and Alfredo Stussi
   (Pisa, 2000), pp. 181–210; see also Rocco Sinisgalli, *Il nuovo 'De
   pictura' di Leon Battista Alberti = The New 'De pictura' of Leon Battista Alberti*
   (Rome, 2006), pp. 25–45.

5 On this see Lucia Bertolini's introduction in Leon Battista Alberti,
   De pictura (redazione volgare), ed. Lucia Bertolini (Florence, 2011),
   pp. 37–58, and especially p. 51 on *De pictura* as an intellectual
   transgression. Also, on the question of the purpose of the
   treatise, see Charles Hope and Elizabeth McGrath, 'Artists and
   Humanists', in *The Cambridge Companion to Renaissance Humanism*, ed.
   Jill Kraye (Cambridge, 1996), pp. 161–88; and Charles Hope,
   'The Structure and Purpose of De pictura', in *Leon Battista Alberti
   e il Quattrocento: studi in onore di Cecil Grayson e Ernst Gombrich. Atti del
   convegno internazionale, Mantova, 29–31 ottobre 1998*, ed. Luca Chiavoni,
   Gianfranco Ferlisi and Maria Vittoria Grassi (Florence, 2001),
   pp. 251–67.

6 Leon Battista Alberti, *On Painting and On Sculpture: The Latin Texts
   of De pictura and De statua*, ed. and trans. Cecil Grayson (London,
   1972), pp. 37, 39.

7 Ibid., p. 41.

8 Ibid., p. 37; and Alberti, *De pictura (redazione volgare)*, pp. 205–6.
   In the Latin, the phrase is 'pinguiore . . . Minerva'.

9 For a concise discussion of the development of perspective,
   including the contribution of Brunelleschi, Alberti and others,
   see Jules Lubbock, *Storytelling in Christian Art from Giotto to Donatello*
   (London, 2006), pp. 175–90.

10 I have modified the translation, based on the vernacular. See
   Alberti, *On Painting*, pp. 60–61; Alberti, *De pictura (redazione volgare)*,
   p. 250.

11 I have modified the translation, based on the vernacular. See
   Alberti, *On Painting*, p. 63; Alberti, *De pictura (redazione volgare)*, p. 252:
   'ma di nuovo fabrichiamo un'arte di pittura'.

12 Alberti, *On Painting*, pp. 67–9.

13 Ibid., p. 89.

14 Ibid., pp. 70–71.

15 For a full and nuanced discussion of the range of significance of the two terms, see Anthony Grafton, '*Historia* and *Istoria*: Alberti's Terminology in Context', *I Tatti Studies*, VIII (1999), pp. 37–68.

16 Alberti, *On Painting*, pp. 72–3. On this see James Hall, *Michelangelo and the Reinvention of the Human Body* (New York, 2005), p. 41.

17 Alberti, *On Painting*, pp. 72–3.

18 This admonition regarding inappropriate mixtures derives from a well-known passage in Horace, *Ars poetica*, 1.1–13.

19 Alberti, *On Painting*, p. 75.

20 Ibid., p. 81.

21 Michael Baxandall, *Giotto and the Orators: Humanist Observers of Painting in Italy and the Discovery of Pictorial Composition, 1350–1450* (Oxford, 1971, reprinted 2006), p. 131.

22 On this see ibid., pp. 135–9.

23 Gerhard Wolf, 'The Body and Antiquity in Alberti's Art Theoretical Writings', in *Antiquity and Its Interpreters*, ed. Alina Payne, Anne Kuttner and Rebekah Smick (Cambridge, 2000), pp. 174–90, here 175. Hope and McGrath, 'Artists and Humanists', p. 165, point out that Alberti's treatise follows Quintilian's tripartite division of *ars* (art), *opus* (work) and *artifex* (artist).

24 Alberti, *On Painting*, p. 65.

25 I have modified the translation, based on the vernacular. See Alberti, *On Painting*, p. 83; and Alberti, *De pictura (redazione volgare)*, p. 282.

26 Alberti, *On Painting*, pp. 57–8.

27 Ibid., pp. 75–7.

28 Ibid., p. 83.

29 Leon Battista Alberti, *Opere volgari*, ed. Cecil Grayson (Bari, 1960–66), vol. II, pp. 161–2.

30 On the mosaic metaphor in general see Eric McPhail, 'The Mosaic of Speech: A Classical Topos in Renaissance Aesthetics', *Journal of the Warburg and Courtauld Institutes*, LXVI (2003), pp. 249–64.

31 *De ordine*, 1.2.2. I have used the translation in St Augustine, *On Order [De ordine]*, trans. Silvano Borruso (South Bend, IN, 2007), p. 5.

4 The Self

1 For an excellent summary of the extensive scholarship relating
   to the building, see Alberto Giorgio Cassani, 'Alberti a Rimini.
   Il Tempio della buona e della cattiva fortuna', in *Leon Battista Alberti
   architetto*, ed. Giorgio Grassi and Luciano Patetta (Florence, 2005),
   pp. 153–209.

2 For a detailed analysis of the use of coloured stones at the Tempio
   Malatestiano, including the ovals, see Fabio Barry, *Painting in Stone:
   Architecture and the Poetics of Marble from Antiquity to the Enlightenment*
   (New Haven, CT, 2020), pp. 245–7. On the possible influence
   of San Marco on the form of the facade see Howard Burns,
   'Leon Battista Alberti', in *Storia dell'architettura italiana. Il Quattrocento*,
   ed. Francesco Paolo Fiore (Milan, 1998), p. 133.

3 Burns, 'Leon Battista Alberti', p. 132.

4 On Sigismondo Malatesta and his court see Anthony D'Elia, *Pagan
   Virtue in a Christian World: Sigismondo Malatesta and the Italian Renaissance*
   (Cambridge, MA, 2016).

5 Ibid., pp. 1–29.

6 Cassani, 'Alberti a Rimini', p. 155.

7 Leon Battista Alberti, *On Painting and On Sculpture: The Latin Texts
   of De pictura and De statua*, ed. and trans. Cecil Grayson (London,
   1972), p. 54; and Leon Battista Alberti, *De pictura (redazione volgare)*,
   ed. Lucia Bertolini (Florence, 2011), pp. 236–7. Although Italian
   is able to indicate the first person through verb conjugation alone,
   it is notable that the personal pronoun *io* (I) appears four times
   in this passage, and *mi* (for the reflexive construction *mi piaccino*)
   once: 'Qui solo, lassato l'altre cose, dirò quello fo io quando
   dipingo. *Principio*, dove io debbo dipingere scrivo uno quadrangolo
   di retti angoli quanto grande io voglio, el quale reputo essere una
   finestra aperta per donde io miri quello che quivi sarà dipinto;
   e quivi ditermino quanto mi piaccino nella mia pittura uomini
   grandi.'

8 I have slightly modified the translation. See Alberti, *On Painting*,
   pp. 61–3; and Alberti, *De pictura (redazione volgare)*, pp. 250–51.

9 Ovid, *Metamorphoses*, 3.337–508, provides one of the best known
   versions.

10 On this see Mary Pardo, 'On the Identity of "Masaccio" in L. B. Alberti's Dedication of *Della pittura*', in *Perspectives on Early Modern and Modern Intellectual History: Essays in Honour of Nancy S. Struever*, ed. Joseph Marino and Melinda W. Schlitt (Rochester, NY, 2001), pp. 223–58.

11 On this and other bronze portraits of Alberti see Joanna Woods-Marsden, *Renaissance Self-portraiture: The Visual Construction of Identity and the Social Status of the Artist* (New Haven, CT, 1998), pp. 71–7; and the entries by Cristina Acidini and Bruna Maria Tomasello in Cristina Acidini and Gabriele Morolli, eds, *L'uomo del Rinascimento: Leon Battista Alberti e le arti a Firenze tra ragione e bellezza*, exh. cat., Palazzo Strozzi, Florence (2006), pp. 62–5.

12 Martin McLaughlin, 'From Lepidus to Leon Battista Alberti: Naming, Renaming, and Anonymizing the Self in Quattrocento Italy', *Romance Studies*, XXXI/3–4 (2013), pp. 152–66, here 153.

13 Woods-Marsden, *Renaissance Self-portraiture*, p. 74.

14 Mark Jarzombek, *On Leon Baptista Alberti: His Literary and Aesthetic Theories* (Cambridge, MA, 1989), pp. 51–9.

15 Leon Battista Albert, *Dinner Pieces*, trans. David Marsh (Binghamton, N\, 1987), p. 16.

16 Ibid., pp. 16–18.

17 Anthony Grafton, *Leon Battista Alberti: Master Builder of the Italian Renaissance* (New York, 2000), pp. 23–4.

18 Renée Neu Watkins, 'Leon Battista Alberti in the Mirror: An Interpretation of the *Vita* with a New Translation', *Italian Quarterly*, XXX/117 (1989), p. 7.

19 Ibid., p. 8.

20 Ibid., p. 15.

21 Ibid., p. 9.

22 Stephen Greenblatt, *Renaissance Self-fashioning: From More to Shakespeare* (London, 1980, reprinted 2005).

23 Watkins, 'Leon Battista Alberti in the Mirror', p. 9.

24 Ibid., p. 11.

25 Ibid., p. 7.

26 Christopher S. Celenza, *Renaissance Humanism and the Papal Curia: Lapo da Castiglionchio the Younger's 'De curiae commodis'* (Ann Arbor, MI, 1999), pp. 156–7.

27 Cristoforo Landino, *Scritti critici e teorici*, ed. Roberto Cardini
    (Rome, 1974), vol. I, p. 120: 'Tornami alla mente lo stilo di Battista
    Alberto, el quale come nuova cameleonta sempre quello colore
    piglia el quale è nella cosa della quale scrive.'
28 Alberti, *De pictura (redazione volgare)*, p. 217: 'e questi fanno quanto
    si dice il cameleone, animale che piglia d'ogni a sé prossima cosa
    colore.'
29 Alberti, *On Painting*, pp. 42–3: 'Atque hi quidem radii id agunt quod
    aiunt camaleonta animal et huiusmodi feras metu conterritas solere
    propinquarum rerum colores suscipere ne a venatoribus facile
    reperiantur.'
30 The Latin text, ed. Donatella Coppini, with an Italian translation
    by M. Letizia Bracciali Magnini, notes and bibliography can be
    found in Leon Battista Alberti, *Opere latine*, ed. Roberto Cardini
    (Rome, 2010), pp. 1017–38.
31 Ibid., p. 1020.
32 Alberti, *Dinner Pieces*, p. 213.
33 Ibid., p. 215.

5 The Family

1 In 1386 the Alberti contributed a brigade of knights to a civic
   procession, decking them out in fine outfits and displaying the
   family, rather than the communal, insignia. This act provoked
   widespread outrage and was perhaps as great a miscalculation
   as their attempt to install Filippo Magalotti as Gonfaloniere
   di Giustizia. On this see John M. Najemy, *A History of Florence,
   1200–1575* (Malden, MA, 2006), p. 186.
2 On the Alberti properties, see Brenda Preyer, '"Da chasa gli
   Alberti": The "Territory" and Housing of the Family', in *Leon
   Battista Alberti: Architetture e Committenti. Atti dei Convegni internazionali
   del Comitato nazionale VI centenario della nascita di Leon Battista Alberti:
   Firenze, Rimini, Mantova, 12–16 October 2004*, ed. Arturo Calzona et al.
   (Florence, 2009), vol. I, pp. 3–34.
3 For a discussion of the problem, which argues for a later date for
   the facade, and which concludes that Alberti was not the architect,
   see Charles Mack, 'The Rucellai Palace: Some New Proposals',

Art Bulletin, LVI/4 (1974), pp. 517–29. For a counter argument, and a very comprehensive account of the building, see Brenda Preyer, 'The Rucellai Palace', in F. W. Kent, et al., *Giovanni Rucellai ed il suo Zibaldone*, vol. II: *A Florentine Patrician and His Palace* (London, 1981), pp. 155–225, especially pp. 189–93. The debate has been continued by scholars on both sides of the argument.

4   Preyer, 'The Rucellai Palace', pp. 179–84.

5   Ibid., p. 189; and Massimo Bulgarelli, *Leon Battista Alberti, 1404–1472: Architettura e storia* (Milan, 2008), pp. 47–51.

6   The claim was made by the humanist and some-time curialist Paolo Cortesi. See Kathleen Weil-Garris and John F. D'Amico, *The Renaissance Cardinal's Ideal Palace: A Chapter from Cortesi's 'De cardinalatu'* (Rome, 1980), pp. 86–7.

7   F. W. Kent, *Household and Lineage in Renaissance Florence: The Family of the Capponi, Ginori, and Rucellai* (Princeton, NJ, 1977), p. 285.

8   The text is contained in *Giovanni Rucellai ed il suo Zibaldone*, vol. I: *il Zibaldone Quaresimale*, ed. Alessandro Perosa (London, 1960).

9   Carlo Ceschi, 'La madre di Leon Battista Alberti', *Bollettino d'arte*, XXXIII (1948), pp. 191–2.

10 Girolamo Mancini, *Vita di Leon Battista Alberti*, 2nd edn (Florence, 1911), pp. 24–5.

11 For the letter see Alberti, *Corpus epistolare e documentario di Leon Battista Alberti*, ed. Paola Benigni, Roberto Cardini and Mariangela Regoliosi (Florence, 2007), 'scheda' I, pp. 76–7.

12 Gary R. Grund, trans. and ed., *Humanist Comedies* (Cambridge, MA, 2005), p. 75.

13 Leon Battista Alberti, *The Use and Abuse of Books: De commodis litterarum atque incommodis*, trans. Renée Neu Watkins (Prospect Heights, N\, 1999), p. 15.

14 This history is detailed in Paola Benigni, 'Tra due testamenti: riflessioni su alcuni aspetti problematici della biografia albertiana', in *Il testamento di Leon Battista Alberti: il manoscritto Statuti Mss. 87 della Biblioteca del Senato della Repubblica 'Giovanni Spadolini': i tempi, i luoghi, i protagonisti*, ed. Enzo Bentivoglio (Rome, 2005), pp. 73–80, here 73–4.

15 Renée Neu Watkins, 'Leon Battista Alberti in the Mirror: An Interpretation of the *Vita* with a New Translation', *Italian Quarterly*, XXX/117 (1989), p. 9.

16 Ibid.

17 Mancini, *Vita*, p. 169. The letter, dating from 1436, is addressed
    to Benedetto di Bernardo Alberti by Filippo di Giovanni di Ser
    Rucco, who managed Benedetto's interests in Florence.

18 Watkins, 'Leon Battista Alberti in the Mirror', p. 8.

19 Leon Battista Alberti, *Dinner Pieces*, trans. David Marsh
    (Binghamton, N\, 1987), p. 17.

20 Benigni, 'Tra due testamenti', p. 75.

21 A detailed account of the structure and the collapse of these
    banking businesses is given in Luca Boschetto, *Leon Battista Alberti e
    Firenze: biografia, storia, letteratura* (Florence, 2000), pp. 20–63.

22 For the quotation see Benigni, 'Tra due testamenti', p. 76. For the
    standing of the Alberti in Florence following the collapse, see
    Boschetto, *Leon Battista Alberti e Firenze*, pp. 63–7.

23 Boschetto, *Leon Battista Alberti e Firenze*, p. 76.

24 See Bertolini's introduction in Leon Battista Alberti, *De pictura
    (redazione volgare)*, ed. Lucia Bertolini (Florence, 2011), pp. 40–41.

25 Watkins, 'Leon Battista Alberti in the Mirror', p. 8.

26 Ibid., p. 10.

27 Leon Battista Alberti, *The Albertis of Florence: Leon Battista Alberti's Della
    famiglia*, trans. Guido A. Guarino (Lewisburg, PA, 1971), pp. 39–40.

28 Ibid., p. 162.

29 Leon Battista Alberti, *Opere volgari*, ed. Cecil Grayson (Bari,
    1960–66), vol. I, p. 163.

30 Alberti, *The Albertis of Florence*, p. 205.

31 Ibid., p. 214. I have slightly modified the translation.

32 Alberti, *Opere volgari*, vol. I, p. 192.

33 Boschetto, *Leon Battista Alberti e Firenze*, pp. 58–9.

34 On this see Martin McLaughlin, 'Leon Battista Alberti and the
    Redirection of Renaissance Humanism', *Proceedings of the British
    Academy*, CLXVII (2010), p. 38.

35 The Latin text, ed. Mariangela Regoliosi, with an Italian
    translation by M. Letizia Bracciali Magnini, notes and
    bibliography can be found in Leon Battista Alberti, *Opere latine*,
    ed. Roberto Cardini (Rome, 2010), pp. 961–86. For a recent
    analysis of the *Canis*, see Martin McLaughlin, *Leon Battista Alberti.
    La vita, l'umanesimo, le opera letterarie* (Florence, 2016), pp. 71–96.

36 On this, see the entry by Paola Massalin in Cristina Acidini and Gabriele Morolli, eds, *L'uomo del Rinascimento: Leon Battista Alberti e le arti a Firenze tra ragione e bellezza*, exh. cat., Palazzo Strozzi, Florence (2006), p. 75; and the entry by Lucia Bertolini in Alberti, *Corpus epistolare*, 'scheda' 13, pp. 164–76; as well as Martin McLaughlin, 'From Lepidus to Leon Battista Alberti: Naming, Renaming, and Anonymizing the Self in Quattrocento Italy', *Romance Studies*, XXXI/3–4 (2013), p. 153.

37 For the division of the palace, and a reconstruction of the spaces, see Brenda Preyer, 'Il palazzo di messer Benedetto degli Alberti, e di Leon Battista', in *Il testamento di Leon Battista Alberti: il manoscritto Statuti Mss. 87 della Biblioteca del Senato della Repubblica 'Giovanni Spadolini': i tempi, i luoghi, i protagonisti*, ed. Enzo Bentivoglio (Rome, 2005), pp. 89–92.

38 John M. Najemy, *A History of Florence, 1200–1575* (Malden, MA, 2006), p. 7.

39 Giovanni Villani, *Nuova Cronica* (Parma, 1990), vol. I, bk II, chap. XX, p. 84.

40 'Purgatorio', XII, 100–107.

41 Alberti, *Opere volgari*, vol. II, p. 187.

42 Giorgio Vasari, *Le vite de' più eccellenti pittori, scultori e architettori, nelle redazioni del 1550 e 1568*, ed. Rosanna Bettarini, with commentary by Paola Barocchi (Florence, 1966–97), vol. III (testo), p. 289. This assumes that Vasari mistakenly identified the bridge as the Ponte alla Carraia.

43 Alberti, *Opere volgari*, vol. II, p. 204.

6 The City

1 Charles M. Rosenberg, *The Este Monuments and Urban Development in Renaissance Ferrara* (Cambridge, 1997), pp. 3, 33–4.

2 Ibid., p. 36.

3 For a rich account of both Ferrarese humanism and Alberti's courtship of Este patronage, see Anthony Grafton, *Leon Battista Alberti: Master Builder of the Italian Renaissance* (New York, 2000), pp. 189–224.

4 On the Niccolò III monument and the competition, see
   Rosenberg, *The Este Monuments*, pp. 50–82; Grafton, *Leon Battista Alberti*, pp. 216–19.

5 Leon Battista Alberti, *De equo animante = Il cavallo vivo*, trans.
   Antonio Videtta (Naples, 1991), pp. 82–5.

6 Rosenberg, *The Este Monuments*, pp. 68–70.

7 Ibid., pp. 14–20, 35.

8 Ibid., pp. 22, 33.

9 Alberti makes this claim in his book of mathematical games, *Ex ludis rerum mathematicarum*, written for Leonello's brother Meliaduse d'Este. See Leon Battista Alberti, *The Mathematical Works of Leon Battista Alberti*, ed. Kim Williams et al. (Basel, 2010), pp. 40–41.

10 See Joseph Rykwert's introduction in Leon Battista Alberti, *On the Art of Building in Ten Books*, trans. Joseph Rykwert, Neil Leach and Robert Tavernor (Cambridge, MA, 1988), p. xviii.

11 For this discussion see Alberti, *On the Art of Building*, bk V, chap. 1, pp. 117–19.

12 Manfredo Tafuri, *Ricerca del Rinascimento* (Turin, 1992), p. 22.

13 Alberti, *On the Art of Building*, bk V, chap. 3, p. 122.

14 For translations and a discussion of the names see Timothy Kircher, *Living Well in Renaissance Italy: The Virtues of Humanism and the Irony of Leon Battista Alberti* (Tempe, AZ, 2012), p. 116.

15 Leon Battista Alberti, *Opere volgari*, ed. Cecil Grayson (Bari, 1960–66), vol. II, p. 79.

16 Renée Neu Watkins, 'Leon Battista Alberti in the Mirror: An Interpretation of the *Vita* with a New Translation', *Italian Quarterly*, XXX/117 (1989), p. 8.

17 Petrarch, *Canzoniere*, 237, line 15: 'poi ch'Amore femmi un cittadin de' Boschi.'

18 On this see William M. Bowsky, 'Medieval Citizenship: The Individual and the State in the Commune of Siena, 1287–1355', in *Studies in Medieval and Renaissance History*, ed. William M. Bowsky (Lincoln, NE, 1967), vol. IV, pp. 195–243, here 210–11. On the connections between sylvan citizens and Petrarch's self-identification as an exile and citizen of the woods, see Laurence E. Hooper, 'Exile and Petrarch's Reinvention of Authorship', *Renaissance Quarterly*, LXIX/4 (2006), pp. 1227–8.

19 For a good summary and analysis, including the argument that the
    Stoic remedies are presented as insufficient, see Annalisa Ceron,
    'Leon Battista Alberti's Care of the Self as Medicine of the Mind:
    A First Glance at *Theogenius, Profugiorum ab erumna libri III*, and Two
    Related *Intercenales*', *Journal of Early Modern Studies*, IV/2 (2015),
    pp. 9–36.

20 The relevant passages are in Alberti, *Opere volgari*, vol. II, pp. 151–2.

21 Christine Smith, *Architecture in the Culture of Early Humanism: Ethics,
    Aesthetics and Eloquence, 1400–1470* (New York, 1992), pp. 3–18 and
    80–97.

22 Alberti, *Opere volgari*, vol. II, p. 45.

23 See Mirko Tavoni, *Latino, grammatica, volgare: Storia di una questione
    umanistica* (Padua, 1984); and for some recent discussions, including
    useful bibliographic information, Andrea Rizzi and Eva Soldato,
    'Latin and Vernacular in Quattrocento Florence and Beyond:
    An Introduction', and Andrea Rizzi, 'Leonardo Bruni and the
    Shimmering Facets of Languages in Early Quattrocento Florence',
    both in *I Tatti Studies in the Italian Renaissance*, XVI/1–2 (September
    2013), pp. 231–42 and 243–56 respectively.

24 Alberti, *Opere volgari*, vol. III, pp. 175–93.

25 See Guglielmo Gorni, 'Storia del certame coronario', *Rinascimento*,
    n.s. XII (1972), pp. 135–81; and Grafton, *Leon Battista Alberti*,
    pp. 171–4. On the *Certame* see also Lucia Bertolini, *De vera amicitia:
    i testi del primo Certame coronario* (Modena, 1993).

26 Leon Battista Alberti, *Rime / Poèmes, suivis de la Protesta / Protestation*,
    ed. Guglielmo Gorni, trans. (French) M. Sabbatini (Paris, 2002),
    pp. 220–33.

27 *Ibid.*; and Grafton, *Leon Battista Alberti*, p. 173.

7 Technology and Folly

1 Stefano Borsi, *Leon Battista Alberti e Roma* (Florence, 2003), p. 98.

2 Poggio Bracciolini, *De varietate fortunae* (Helsinki, 1993).

3 On this episode see Girolamo Mancini, *Vita di Leon Battista Alberti*,
   2nd edn (Florence, 1911), pp. 278–81; Anthony Grafton, *Leon
   Battista Alberti: Master Builder of the Italian Renaissance* (New York,
   2000), pp. 248–52.

4 On Nemi and its cult see James George Frazer, *The Golden Bough: A Study in Magic and Religion. A New Abridgement from the Second and Third Editions*, ed. Robert Fraser (Oxford, 1994), pp. 9–21.

5 Leon Battista Alberti, *On the Art of Building in Ten Books*, trans. Joseph Rykwert, Neil Leach and Robert Tavernor (Cambridge, MA, 1988), bk 5, chap. 12, p. 136. Alberti directs the reader to his treatise *The Ship*, which is now lost.

6 Leon Battista Alberti, *The Mathematical Works of Leon Battista Alberti*, ed. Kim Williams, Lionel March and Stephen R. Wassell (Basel, 2010), p. 10.

7 On this, and on Alberti's wider opposition to illustrations, see Francesco Furlan's introductory essay in Leon Battista Alberti, *Leon Battista Alberti's Delineation of the City of Rome (Desciptio Urbis Romae)*, ed. Mario Carpo and Francesco Furlan, trans. Peter Hicks (Tempe, AZ, 2007), pp. 19–27.

8 Alberti, *The Mathematical Works*, p. 51 (I have slightly modified the translation, making *terra* 'city' rather than 'place').

9 On this see Stephen R. Wassell's commentary on the game, ibid., pp. 122–6.

10 Alberti, *Leon Battista Alberti's Delineation*, p. 97.

11 Ibid., p. viii.

12 Ibid., p. 16.

13 Leon Battista Alberti, *Dinner Pieces*, trans. David Marsh (Binghamton, N\, 1987), p. 58.

14 Tafuri's essay was later included in his *Interpreting the Renaissance: Princes, Cities, Architects*, trans. Daniel Sherer (New Haven, CT, 2006), pp. 23–58.

15 On the likely complexity of Alberti's position see Borsi, *Leon Battista Alberti e Roma*, pp. 106, 260–61.

16 Leon Battista Alberti, *Momus*, ed. Virginia Brown and Sarah Knight, trans. Sarah Knight (Cambridge, MA, 2003), p. 75.

17 Ibid., p. 13.

18 Christine Smith, 'The Apocalypse Sent Up: A Parody of the Papacy by Leon Battista Alberti', *MLN*, CXIX/1 (2004), S162–S177.

19 Alberti, *Momus*, pp. 309–11.

20 Ibid., p. 105.

21 On unmasking in art, in this case in relation to Bruegel, see Joseph
    Leo Koerner, *Bosch and Bruegel: From Enemy Painting to Everyday Life*
    (Princeton, NJ, 2016), pp. 318–27.
22 The remark occurs towards the start of Alberti's treatise on
    cryptography where he recalls a conversation with Leonardo Dati.
    See Leon Battista Alberti, *Dello scrivere in cifra* [*De componendis cyfris*]
    (Turin, 1994), p. 28.
23 Renée Neu Watkins, 'Leon Battista Alberti in the Mirror: An
    Interpretation of the *Vita* with a New Translation', *Italian Quarterly*,
    XXX/117 (2013), p. 10.
24 Alberti, *Momus*, p. 191.

8 Architecture

 1 See the wide-ranging discussion of *De re aedificatoria* in Françoise
    Choay, *The Rule and the Model: On the Theory of Architecture and Urbanism*,
    ed. Denise Bratton, trans. MIT (Cambridge, MA, 1997), especially
    pp. 16–33 and 115–35.
 2 Howard Burns, 'Leon Battista Alberti', in *Storia dell'architettura
    italiana. Il Quattrocento*, ed. Francesco Paolo Fiore (Milan, 1998),
    pp. 114–65, here 114 (my translation).
 3 Leon Battista Alberti, *On the Art of Building in Ten Books*, trans. Joseph
    Rykwert, Neil Leach and Robert Tavernor (Cambridge, MA,
    1988), p. 3.
 4 On this see Burns, 'Leon Battista Alberti', especially p. 123;
    Nikolaus Pevsner, 'The Term "Architect" in the Middle Ages',
    Speculum, XVII/4 (October 1942), pp. 549–62; and Cristina Eusebi,
    'Contributo dell'italiano alla formazione del lessico architettonico
    rinascimentale inglese', PhD thesis, Università degli Studi di
    Trento, 2012, pp. 6–42.
 5 Alberti, *On the Art of Building*, p. 5.
 6 Ibid., p. 7.
 7 On *lineamenta* as shape, and on their instantiation in drawings and
    buildings, see Branko Mitrović, *Serene Greed of the Eye: Leon Battista
    Alberti and the Philosophical Foundations of Renaissance Architectural Theory*
    (Munich, 2005), pp. 30–39, 49–58, 177–83.
 8 Alberti, *On the Art of Building*, p. 9.

9   Ibid., p. 61.
10 Ibid., p. 89.
11 Ibid., p. 154.
12 Ibid., p. 155.
13 Ibid., p. 156.
14 Mitrović, *Serene Greed*, p. 118; Aristotle, *Nichomachean Ethics*, 1106b, 9–35.
15 Quintilian, *Institutio oratoria*, 1.5.
16 Quoted in Jacques Le Goff, *Saint Francis of Assisi*, trans. Christine Rhone (London, 2004), p. 19.
17 Alberti, *On the Art of Building*, p. 156.
18 On this see Elisabetta Di Stefano, *L'altro sapere: Bello, arte, imagine in Leon Battista Alberti* (Palermo, 2000), pp. 46–50.
19 Christine Smith, *Architecture in the Culture of Early Humanism: Ethics, Aesthetics and Eloquence, 1400–1470* (New York, 1992), p. 80 (and pp. 57–69 for her discussion of Alberti's attitude towards gothic architecture).
20 On this see Alina Payne, *The Architectural Treatise in the Italian Renaissance: Architectural Invention, Ornament, and Literary Culture* (Cambridge, 1999), pp. 72–88. I have adopted Payne's terms here.
21 Alberti, *On the Art of Building*, p. 310.
22 Władysław Tatarkiewicz, 'The Great Theory of Beauty and Its Decline', *Journal of Aesthetics and Art Criticism*, XXXI/2 (Winter 1972), pp. 165–80, here 167; see also Massimo Bulgarelli, *Leon Battista Alberti, 1404–1472: Architettura e storia* (Milan, 2008), pp. 12–14.
23 Alberti, *On the Art of Building*, pp. 302–3.
24 Leon Battista Alberti, *Momus*, ed. Virginia Brown and Sarah Knight, trans. Sarah Knight (Cambridge, MA, 2003), pp. 303, 311–13. See also Alberto Giorgio Cassani, 'Et flores quidem negligitis: Saxa admirabimur? Sul coflitto natura-architettura in L. B. Alberti', *Albertiana*, VIII (2005), pp. 57–83; and Caspar Pearson, *Humanism and the Urban World: Leon Battista Alberti and the Renaissance City* (University Park, PA, 2011), pp. 174–7.
25 Bulgarelli, *Leon Battista Alberti*, p. 12.
26 Ibid., pp. 12–14.
27 A compelling case is made in this regard in Marvin Trachtenberg, *Building-in-time: From Giotto to Alberti and Modern Oblivion* (New Haven,

CT, 2010), especially pp. 357–83. See also Choay, *The Rule and the Model*, p. 134, where Alberti is characterized as fashioning an 'architect-hero' who dwells 'outside of time and yet is immersed in its flow'.

28 Luigi Passerini, *Gli Alberti di Firenze; genealogia, storia, e documenti* (Florence, 1869), vol. II, p. 145.

29 For a complete facsimile and translation of the letter, see Robert Tavernor, *On Alberti and the Art of Building* (New Haven, CT, 1998), pp. 59–61. I have modified the translation slightly. For a transcription and a re-reading of this and other relevant documents, see Charles Hope, 'The Early History of the Tempio Malatestiano', *Journal of the Warburg and Courtauld Institutes*, LV (1992), pp. 51–154.

30 Alberti, *On the Art of Building*, p. 305.

31 On this see Bulgarelli, *Leon Battista Alberti*, p. 25.

32 On the mask in relation to the Tempio Malatestiano, see Alberto Giorgio Cassani, 'Per foramina obductae personae. Una fonte per la facciata del Malatestiano', *Albertiana*, V (2002), pp. 61–76.

33 Brenda Preyer, 'The Palazzo Rucellai', in F. W. Kent, et al., *Giovanni Rucellai ed il suo Zibaldone*, vol. II: *A Florentine Patrician and His Palace* (London, 1981), pp. 180, 185–6.

34 Alberti, *Momus*, p. 63; see also Bulgarelli, *Leon Battista Alberti*, p. 19.

35 On Alberti's unsettling of readers, see Timothy Kircher, *Living Well in Renaissance Italy: The Virtues of Humanism and the Irony of Leon Battista Alberti* (Tempe, AZ, 2012), p. 6.

36 On the combination of sources, see Riccardo Pacciani, 'Alberti a Firenze. Una presenza difficile', in *Leon Battista Alberti architetto*, ed. Giorgio Grassi and Luciano Patetta (Florence, 2005), pp. 211–61, here 218; and Bulgarelli, *Leon Battista Alberti*, p. 37.

37 On this idea about art and time see Alexander Nagel and Christopher S. Wood, *Anachronic Renaissance* (New York, 2010), pp. 1–19.

38 See Marco Dezzi Bardeschi, 'Il complesso monumentale di San Pancrazio a Firenze ed il suo restauro (nuovi documenti)', *Quaderni dell'Istituto di Storia dell'architettura*, XIII/73–8 (1966), pp. 1–66, here 41, n. 54; and Tavernor, *On Alberti*, pp. 79, 221, n. 9.

39 Giorgio Vasari, *Le vite de' più eccellenti pittori, scultori e architettori, nelle redazioni del 1550 e 1568*, ed. Rosanna Bettarini, with commentary

   by Paola Barocchi (Florence, 1966–97), vol. III (testo),
   pp. 286, 289.

40　Girolamo Mancini, *Vita di Leon Battista Alberti*, 2nd edn (Florence,
　　1911), p. 461. For the refutation see Lorenzo Amato, 'Sui Primi
　　Documenti di Attribuzione della Facciata di Santa Maria Novella',
　　Medioevo e Rinascimento, XXI/n.s. XVIII (2007), pp. 121–40.

41　For an overview see Ferruccio Canali, 'La facciata di Santa Maria
　　Novella', in *L'uomo del Rinascimento: Leon Battista Alberti e le arti a Firenze
　　tra ragione e bellezza*, ed. Cristina Acidini and Gabriele Morolli,
　　exh. cat., Palazzo Strozzi, Florence (Florence, 2006), pp. 195–9.
　　For examples of two opposing ways of interpreting the evidence
　　regarding Alberti as an architect more broadly, see Burns, 'Leon
　　Battista Alberti'; and Trachtenberg, *Bulding-in-time*, p. 377.

42　Marco Dezzi Bardeschi, *La facciata di Santa Maria Novella a Firenze*
　　(Pisa, 1970), p. 19.

43　Burns, 'Leon Battista Alberti', pp. 138–9.

44　Fabio Barry, *Painting in Stone: Architecture and the Poetics of Marble from
　　Antiquity to the Enlightenment* (New Haven, CT, 2020), p. 249.

45　See Tavernor, *On Alberti*, pp. 115–19.

46　For a rich discussion of the Renaissance palace facade, including
　　the Palazzo Rucellai, as a complex semantic field, see Charles
　　Burroughs, *The Italian Renaissance Palace Facade: Structures of Authority,
　　Surfaces of Sense* (Cambridge, 2002).

47　Anthony Grafton, *Leon Battista Alberti: Master Builder of the Italian
　　Renaissance* (New York, 2000), pp. 184–5; and Caspar Pearson,
　　'The Return of the Giants: Leon Battista Alberti's Letter to
　　Filippo Brunelleschi', *Journal of the Warburg and Courtauld Institutes*,
　　LXXXIII (2019), pp. 113–41.

48　For a close reading of the documents relating to the construction
　　of the church, see Arturo Calzona and Livio Volpi Ghirardini, *Il
　　San Sebastiano di Leon Battista Alberti* (Florence, 1994), pp. 3–86, with
　　the documents themselves transcribed on pp. 141–204. For an
　　accessible account in English, see Tavernor, *On Alberti*, pp. 127–42.
　　My account broadly follows Tavernor's.

49　This is the view of Tavernor, *On Alberti*, p. 136.

50　On the extensive scholarly speculation regarding the status of the
　　'crypt' and its absence from Labacco's drawing, see Arturo Calzona,

'Ludovico Gonzaga, Leon Battista Alberti, Luca Fancelli e il problema della cripta di San Sebastiano', in *Leon Battista Alberti*, ed. Anne Engel and Joseph Rykwert, exh. cat., Palazzo Te, Mantua (Milan, 1994), pp. 225–75.

51 Alberti, *On the Art of Building*, p. 196.

52 For the quotation, see Calzona and Volpi Ghirardini, *Il San Sebastiano di Leon Battista Alberti*, p. 191; Tavernor, *On Alberti*, p. 143. On Alberti's relations with figures at the Mantuan court, see David S. Chambers, 'Who were Alberti's Mantuan Friends?', in *Leon Battista Alberti e il Quattrocento: Studi in onore di Cecil Grayson e Ernst Gombrich. Atti del convegno internazionale, Mantova 29–31 ottobre 1998*, ed. Luca Chiavoni, Gianfranco Ferlisi and Maria Vittoria Grassi (Florence, 2001), pp. 25–45.

53 *Giovanni Rucellai ed il suo Zibaldone*, vol. 1: *il Zibaldone Quaresimale*, ed. Alessandro Perosa (London, 1960), p. 73.

54 Tavernor, *On Alberti*, p. 159.

55 A detailed building history, with transcriptions of the relevant documents, can be found in Eugene J. Johnson, *S. Andrea in Mantua: The Building History* (University Park, PA, 1975). On the Mantuan context and the importance of the Holy Blood, see Bulgarelli, *Leon Battista Alberti*, pp. 117–61.

56 Ibid., p. 64; I have used, with minor variations, the translation in Tavernor, *On Alberti*, p. 159.

57 Johnson, *S. Andrea*, p. 64; Tavernor, *On Alberti*, p. 159.

58 Tavernor, *On Alberti*, p. 165.

59 Johnson, *S. Andrea*, p. 18.

60 Ibid., pp. 19–20.

61 Rudolf Wittkower, *Architectural Principles in the Age of Humanism*, 3rd edn (London, 1962), pp. 33–56.

62 Barry, *Painting in Stone*, pp. 249–50; Bulgarelli, *Leon Battista Alberti*, pp. 178–87.

63 Alberti, *On the Art of Building*, p. 197.

64 Calzona and Volpi Ghirardini, *Il San Sebastiano*, p. 158.

Epilogue

1   See Paola Benigni, 'Tra due testamenti: riflessioni su alcuni aspetti problematici della biografia albertiana', in *Il testamento di Leon Battista Alberti: il manoscritto Statuti Mss. 87 della Biblioteca del Senato della Repubblica 'Giovanni Spadolini': i tempi, i luoghi, i protagonisti*, ed. Enzo Bentivoglio (Rome, 2005), pp. 77–8 for a summary of these details.

2   Leon Battista Alberti, *Autobiografia e altre opere latine*, ed. Loredana Chines and Andrea Severi (Milan, 2012), p. 474.

3   Sergio Bettini, 'Le proprietà Alberti a Bologna', in *Il testamento di Leon Battista Alberti: il manoscritto Statuti Mss. 87 della Biblioteca del Senato della Repubblica 'Giovanni Spadolini': i tempi, i luoghi, i protagonisti*, ed. Enzo Bentivoglio (Rome, 2005), pp. 93–4, here 93. See also Girolamo Mancini, 'Il teastamento di L. B. Alberti', *Archivio storico italiano*, II/72 (1914), pp. 20–52.

4   Alberto Giorgio Cassani, 'Alberti a Rimini. Il Tempio della buona e della cattiva fortuna', in *Leon Battista Alberti architetto*, ed. Giorgio Grassi and Luciano Patetta (Florence, 2005), pp. 153–209, here 183.

5   For a recent discussion of this and other Renaissance portraits see Michel Paoli, 'Les portraits de Leon Battista Alberti des XVe and XVIe siècles', in *Leon Battista Alberti: la biblioteca di un umanista*, ed. Roberto Cardini, Mariangela Rogliosi and Lucia Bertolini (Florence, 2005), pp. 79–86. His hand is reminiscent of the 'manicules' so beloved of Renaissance readers. On this see William H. Sherman, *Used Books: Marking Readers in Renaissance England* (Philadelphia, PA, 2008), pp. 25–52.

6   Alberti, *Autobiografia e altre opere latine*, pp. 472, 473; and Enzo Bentivoglio, 'Per Battista Alberti: *nihil dictum quin prius dictum . . . o quasi*', in *Il testamento di Leon Battista Alberti*, ed. Enzo Bentivoglio (Rome, 2005), pp. 5–7.

SELECT BIBLIOGRAPHY

There has been a great deal of scholarship on Alberti in recent years, especially in Italian. The following bibliography indicates a very small selection of key texts.

Works on Alberti in English

Grafton, Anthony, *Leon Battista Alberti: Master Builder of the Italian Renaissance* (New York, 2000)

Jarzombek, Mark, *On Leon Baptista Alberti: His Literary and Aesthetic Theories* (London, 1989)

Kircher, Timothy, *Living Well in Renaissance Italy: The Virtues of Humanism and the Irony of Leon Battista Alberti* (Tempe, AZ, 2012)

McLaughlin, Martin, 'Leon Battista Alberti and the Redirection of Renaissance Humanism', *Proceedings of the British Academy*, CLXVII (2010), pp. 25–59

Pearson, Caspar, *Humanism and the Urban World: Leon Battista Alberti and the Renaissance City* (University Park, PA, 2011)

Tavernor, Robert, *On Alberti and the Art of Building* (New Haven, CT, 1998)

Works on Alberti in Italian

Borsi, Franco, *Leon Battista Alberti: l'opera completa* (Milan, 1996)

Borsi, Stefano, *Leon Battista Alberti e Roma* (Florence, 2003)

Boschetto, Lucca, *Leon Battista Alberti e Firenze: biografia, storia, letteratura* (Florence, 2000)

Bulgarelli Massimo, *Leon Battista Alberti, 1404–1472: Architettura e Storia* (Milan, 2008)

Cardini, Roberto, *Mosaici: il 'nemico' dell'Alberti* (Rome, 1990)

Mancini, Girolamo, *Vita di Leon Battista Alberti*, 2nd edn (Florence, 1911)

English Translations of Alberti's Works

The Albertis of Florence: Leon Battista Alberti's 'Della famiglia', trans. Guido A. Guarino (Lewisburg, PA, 1971)

Dinner Pieces, trans. David Marsh (Binghamton, NY, 1987)

Il nuovo 'De pictura' di Leon Battista Alberti = The New 'De pictura' of Leon Battista Alberti, ed., with essays and commentary, Rocco Sinisgalli (Rome, 2006)

Leon Battista Alberti's Delineation of the City of Rome (Desciptio Urbis Romae), ed. Mario Carpo and Francesco Furlan, trans. Peter Hicks (Tempe, AZ, 2007)

The Mathematical Works of Leon Battista Alberti, ed. Kim Williams et al. (Basel, 2010)

On the Art of Building in Ten Books, trans. Joseph Rykwert, Neil Leach and Robert Tavernor (Cambridge, MA, 1988)

On Painting and On Sculpture: The Latin Texts of De pictura and De statua, ed. and trans. Cecil Grayson (London, 1972)

The Use and Abuse of Books: De commodis litterarum atque incommodis, trans. Renée Neu Watkins (Prospect Heights, NY, 1999)

Collections of Works in Original Language

Leon Battista Alberti, *Autobiografia e altre opere latine*, ed. Loredana Chines and Andrea Severi (Milan, 2012)

—, *Opere latine*, ed. Roberto Cardini (Rome, 2010)

—, *Opere volgari*, ed. Cecil Grayson, 3 vols (Bari, 1960–73)

Edizione Nazionale delle opere di Leon Battista Alberti, under the auspices of the Centro di Studi sul Classicismo, 12 vols with further vols in progress (Florence, 2004–)

ACKNOWLEDGEMENTS

I began this project and wrote most of the first draft as a member of staff in the School of Philosophy and Art History at the University of Essex and completed it after moving to the Warburg Institute. I am grateful for the good cheer and solidarity of colleagues and students at both institutions during a period that has included lengthy strikes and a global pandemic, among other vicissitudes of fortune. In 2018, I was privileged to stay for a period at the Villa I Tatti in Florence, and I owe particular thanks to the director, Alina Payne, for her support. Martin McLaughlin and Stefano Cracolici gave very generously of their time and read early versions of the manuscript. Their insights and guidance have been invaluable. Colleagues at other institutions, including Gervase Rosser, Nicholas Terpstra, Bronwen Wilson, Elsje van Kessel, Dan Kubis, David Kim, Andrew Leach and Denise Costanzo kindly invited me to speak, allowing me to try out some ideas. Jules Lubbock and Lisa Wade have been long-term supporters. I am grateful to Michael Leaman and François Quiviger for commissioning the book, and to Alex Ciobanu and Phoebe Colley for their work on its production. The ever-brilliant Maria Loh has been a constant source of support and encouragement and has helped in more ways than I can enumerate.

More broadly, I am profoundly in debt to the many scholars who have produced specialist studies on Alberti. I have, out of necessity, kept citations to an absolute minimum, but the range of works discussing Alberti (not to mention translations and critical editions of his writings) is astonishing and their quality is often humbling.

PHOTO ACKNOWLEDGEMENTS

The author and publishers wish to express their thanks to the below sources of illustrative material and/or permission to reproduce it. Some locations of artworks are also given below, in the interest of brevity:

Accademia di belle arti G. Carrara, Bergamo: 41; AdobeStock: 5 and 6 (Enrico Della Pietra), 14 (peisker), 21 (giumas); photos Stephen Bartlett, Kennesaw State University: 9, 58, 62; Basilica di San Clemente, Rome: 11; Biblioteca Nazionale Centrale di Firenze: 30 (MS II.IV.38, fol. 119v); Biblioteca Nazionale Centrale di Roma: 1 (MS V.E. 738, fol. 1vv); Bodleian Libraries, University of Oxford: 27 (MS Canon. Class. Lat. 81, fol. 137r); reproduced by permission of Centro Studi Generazioni e Luoghi – Archivi Alberti La Marmora di Biella: 39; photo Niccolò Chiamori/Unsplash: 48; photo DeAgostini/ G. Dagli Orti via Getty Images: 20; Peter Horree/Alamy Stock Photo: 42; Houghton Library, Harvard University, Cambridge, MA: 50 (MS Typ 316, seq. 60); iStock.com: 32 (anamejia18), 66 (Rimbalzino); courtesy Oliver Matthews: 18, 19; The Metropolitan Museum of Art, New York: 23; The Morgan Library & Museum, New York, photo courtesy The Morgan Library & Museum, New York: 53 (MA 1734, recto; purchase, gift of the Fellows, 1956); Museo dell'Opera del Duomo, Florence: 17; National Gallery of Art, Washington, DC: 24, 29, 31, 46; photos Caspar Pearson: 2, 13, 15, 28, 33, 34, 40, 52, 55, 65; photo Antonio Quattrone/Archivio Quattrone/Mondadori Portfolio via Getty Images: 4; photo Ben Rimmer: 16; photos © Scala, Florence 2022: 36, 57, 64 (courtesy of the Ministero Beni e Att. Culturali e del Turismo); Shutterstock.com: 12 (Renata Sedmakova), 45 (milosk50),

INDEX

Illustration numbers are indicated by *italics*